THE FLEET AIR ARM

This dramatic picture shows one of the training Harriers lifting off the end of a temporary 'ski jump' built for the Farnborough Air Show. Fixed-wing flying in the Royal Navy was officially phased out in the White Paper of 1968, following the cancellation of a new aircraft carrier (CVA01) to replace the *Ark Royal*, in 1966. The Sea Harrier and the new compact aircraft carriers, the *Invincible, Illustrious* and *Ark Royal*, mark the re-introduction of fixed-wing flying in the Service.

THE
FLEET
AIR ARM

A Pictorial History

REGINALD LONGSTAFF

ROBERT HALE LIMITED
LONDON

Copyright © R. Longstaff 1981
© Line drawings Jack White 1981
First published in Great Britain 1981.

ISBN 0 7091 9141 3

Robert Hale Limited
Clerkenwell House
Clerkenwell Green
London EC1R 0HT

Photoset, printed and bound
in Great Britain by
REDWOOD BURN LIMITED
Trowbridge, Wiltshire

Introduction

If the death of HMS *Ark Royal* in December 1978 brought one glorious era to an end in British Naval Aviation, then the introduction of the elevated ramp or 'ski jump' was the birth of a new one with a bright promise for the future. In theory, the ski jump will enable a large number of warships or merchant ships with only short 'flight-decks', to operate the high performance Sea Harrier and its successors. The invention has been compared in importance with those other great British naval inventions of the angled flight-deck, the steam catapult and the mirror landing sight. Until the new aircraft carrier HMS *Invincible* became operational with its elevated ramp and Sea Harriers, the Navy's main strike capability rested with its helicopters. Only the Americans and the French will have strike carriers in commission.

The fleet air arm has survived many battles fought in the political arena before, and the long haul to regain control of their own air arm began shortly after the amalgamation of the Royal Naval Air Service (RNAS) and the Royal Flying Corps (RFC) on 1 April 1918, when the RAF was formed. By 1919, naval air power had been reduced to a pitiful spotter-reconnaissance squadron, the remnants of a torpedo bomber (TB) squadron, and one Flight each of fighters, seaplanes and flying boats.

The first tentative step forward was in 1921 when the Admiralty obtained agreement that naval officers (NOs) should be trained as observers. They formed a Special Observer Section, an event of far-reaching importance in providing a nucleus of highly trained men on which to build for the future. On 4 July 1924, the Committee for Imperial Defence (CID) recommended that all observers in naval aircraft should be NOs and that seventy per cent of pilots should be Royal Navy or Royal Marine officers. Then came the exciting years of 1937–1939 which began on 17 February 1937 with the institution of the Naval Air Branch consisting of officers entered for air duties only, and Rear-Admiral G. C. C. Royle relieved Vice-Admiral N. J. Lawrence as Rear-Admiral Aircraft Carriers. After nearly twenty years of inter-

Service bickering, a political decision was reached on 30 July 1937; this stated that all aircraft borne in warships would come under the administrative control of the Admiralty. On 10 August, Rear-Admiral J. D. R. Cunningham was appointed Assistant Chief of Naval Staff (Air) – ACNS (Air) – with a seat on the Board.

In a sense, my interest in naval aviation began the same year. After preliminary 'square bashing', theory and technical training in the Signal School, Royal Naval Barracks, Portsmouth, I passed out as a Wireless Telegraphist. I was to serve in HMS *Courageous*, the newly-commissioned *Ark Royal* in 1939, and later in the escort carrier HMS *Trumpeter*. I still have a book, *Ships of the Royal Navies* – note the plural – written by Oscar Parkes and published in 1937. It lists HMS *Hermes* as the first ship designed by the Admiralty as an aircraft carrier ". . . to solve the problems of design by a medium-sized, lightly-protected ship, moderately fast with a wide radius of action, relying on screening ships for defence." The writer went on: "All carriers are particularly vulnerable and shell or bomb hits are liable to make the flight-decks unusable, wreck the hangars and explode the vast stores of petrol carried." Also listed were: HMS *Pegasus* (late *Ark Royal*) used for experimental work with launching, platforms and catapults, *Argus*, *Eagle*, *Furious*, *Courageous* and *Glorious*. Building under the 1934 programme was *Ark Royal*, and under the 1936 programme, *Illustrious* and *Victorious*.

Finally, on 28 May 1939, the Admiralty regained full operational control of the Fleet Air Arm, although RAF personnel were to remain for some years. RAF aerodromes were handed back to the FAA, the first since the glorious days of the RNAS. Lee-on-Solent became Headquarters and Flag Officer Naval Air Stations; the first distinguished holder of the Flag was Rear-Admiral R. Bell Davies, VC, one of the few RNAS pioneers to have stayed with the Navy. Other stations were Worthy Down (Winchester), Ford (Sussex), and Donibristle (Fife).

The embryo Air Arm was, however, born in the early days of 1903 when the RN began to think seriously about expanding its horizons for spotting, signalling and reconnaissance, with the help of officers such as Prince Louis of Battenberg, Captains R. Tupper, C. Le G. Egerton and Percy Scott. The brief fledgling days of the RNAS and the later years of a mighty Fleet Air Arm, produced officers and men with a genius for improvisation who brought a pioneering approach to their problems, and led the world with their inventions which are still used by naval air powers all over the world.

As far back as 8 June 1903, when a committee on military ballooning was set up, Rear-Admiral H. Lambton – a veteran of the South African War – was stating that there was a good future for ballooning as an aid to artillery. The committee also noted that the man-lifting kites by S. F. Cody were worthy of considerable attention, and stated their requirements for a 'navigable balloon' – later called a 'blimp' – able to operate at a height of 5,000 ft (1,500 m). On 3 November in the grounds of Alexandra Palace, William Beedle tried out a 'navigable balloon' with a swivelling propeller to vary thrust for steering, and another propeller for driving the ship forward. This unique device led Beedle to collaborate with the famous pioneer airship company of E. T. Willows, and the device was strengthened, improved and given more power. On 5 September 1905, the Willows No. 1 airship made a test flight lasting 85 minutes and reached a height of 120 ft (37 m). On 30 October it was inspected on behalf of the War Office by Colonel J. E. Capper, who later became Superintendent of the Balloon Factory at Farnborough. He thought the airship had considerable potential. A Willow-type non-rigid airship or 'blimp' was to be the first ordered by the Admiralty.

It was, however, Cody's kites which stimulated the interest of the Admiralty and really laid the foundations for a future Royal Naval Air Service. Samuel Franklin Cody was a colourful extrovert whose life style was more flamboyant than any contemporary Hollywood fiction. He was variously a playwright, actor, cowboy, buffalo hunter and designer of kites, airships and aeroplanes. On 6 February he wrote to the Admiralty about a superior type of kite able to lift a man for reconnaissance, signalling or spotting the fall of shot. The letter stated that he had twenty kites available for use and had reached a height of 1,200 ft (365 m) with the ship system. Five weeks later on 12 March 1903, Captain R. Tupper, Assistant Director of Naval Ordnance, watched a demonstration by Cody on Woolwich Common and reported: "... the best type of kite I have seen and I think useful for supporting an aerial wire for wireless telegraphy purposes." On 18 March, Prince Louis recommended that the Navy begin their own experiments and noted among the possibilities: lifting an aerial wire for wireless telegraphy both ashore and afloat, and lifting a man to a considerable height from a ship under way, for reconnaissance. He submitted the following plan for approval:

1. Request Mr Cody to send his apparatus to Portsmouth.
2. Direct the Captain of *Vernon* to carry out trials with the 8-ft kite from a gunboat or destroyer, for lifting an aerial wire.
3. To direct the Captain of *Excellent* to carry out trials at Whale Island

with the man-lifting kite. If successful these could then be repeated from a ship under way.

On 25 March 1903, the Admiralty directed the Commander-in-Chief, HM Ships and Vessels, Portsmouth, to carry out the trials proposed by Lord Louis. The trials started on 30 March with various sizes of kites being sent up for test purposes, and on 31 March further tests took place on Whale Island during which an aerial wire was lifted to a height of 600 ft (180 m). Sea trials were conducted in an old 6,710-ton cruiser, HMS *Hector*, and a 670-ton torpedo boat destroyer, HMS *Starfish*. They ended on 4 April, and on the 7th Captain Egerton reported favourably to Admiralty: ". . . these kites are immensely superior to any previously tried here and even as fitted at present, are perfectly capable of raising an aerial wire . . .". The day before, without waiting for Egerton's report to be circulated, Prince Louis wrote to the First Sea Lord recommending that Cody's patents be purchased and that he be employed as a civilian kiting instructor.

The man-lifting trials also took place at Whale Island and it was reported that on the 13 April one of Cody's sons had reached a height of 500 ft (152 m). Three days later the kites went to sea in HMS *Seahorse*, and the next day in perfect weather a wooden log, weight 140 lb (64 kgm), was sent up and fetched down several times. The series of trials ended on 18 April and in his report to the Admiralty, Captain Percy Scott, who had just taken over command of HMS *Excellent*, wrote: ". . . at present it cannot be said that they can be relied upon for man-lifting either on land or sea, except in very favourable weather, but as the inventor has only been working on them for two years there seems to be no reason why their efficiency should not eventually justify their use for this purpose." He commented favourably on their use for wireless telegraphy and distant signalling.

Cody went 'sky high' however, when he asked the Admiralty a premium of £25,000 for his patents, a salary of £1,250 a year while in office, and, when discharged and if the kites were still satisfactory, a further sum of £25,000. On 20 May, the Admiralty replied that they were unable to accept his offer. They did purchase four sets of kites, however, each being a pilot kite, two lifters, and a carrier with controls and basket. These were supplied to HMS *Majestic, Good Hope, Revenge* and *Doris*.

This is where I begin this pictorial history and, of necessity, it can only be representative of the seventy years I have tried to explore.

I make no apology for a chapter on helicopters in the RN since, at the time of writing, these are the most widely used aircraft in the Navy.

Likewise, dates, personalities and selected incidents are of my own choosing. Although I worked for the Director of Public Relations (Navy) for twelve years, the accuracy of statements made and the interpretation placed on them are entirely my own responsibility.

Farnborough, Hants, 1981   R. Longstaff

Abbreviations

To avoid repetitive use of full titles, I have adopted the following abbreviations throughout the text. Those for decorations are the normal ones in use.

ACA	Admiral Commanding Aircraft
ACNS	Assistant Chief of Naval Staff
AD	Air Department, Admiralty
ADAD	Assistant Director Air Department
A/S	Anti-Submarine
AEW	Airborne Early Warning
ASAC	Assistant Superintendent Aircraft Construction
ASW	Anti-Submarine Warfare
BEF	British Expeditionary Force
CFS	Central Flying School
C-in-C	Commander-in-Chief
CID	Committee for Imperial Defence
CO	Commanding Officer
DAD	Director Air Department (later Director Air Division, Admiralty)
DAS	Director Air Services, Admiralty
E	Engineer
ERA	Engine Room Artificer
F	Fighter
FAA	Fleet Air Arm
FF	Fleet Fighter
FR	Fleet Reconnaissance
FS	Fleet Spotter
FTB	Fleet Torpedo Bomber
FO	Flag Officer
FOFT	Flag Officer Flying Training
FOCAS	Flag Officer Carriers and Amphibious Ships
FONAC	Flag Officer Naval Air Command
FONAS	Flag Officer Naval Air Stations
FORA	Flag Officer Reserve Aircraft
FSR	Fighter Spotter Reconnaissance
HAR/HR	Helicopter Air Rescue
HAS	Helicopter Anti-submarine
HU	Helicopter Utility (Commando-Heavy Lift)
ICA	Inspecting Captain of Aircraft
ICAS	Inspecting Captain of Airships
MAC	Merchant Ship Aircraft Carrier
NF	Night Fighter
NO	Naval Officer

RFA	Royal Fleet Auxiliary
RFC	Royal Flying Corps
RMA	Royal Marine Artillery
RMLI	Royal Marine Light Infantry
RN	Royal Navy
RNAS	Royal Naval Air Service
RNR	Royal Naval Reserve
RNVR	Royal Naval Volunteer Reserve
R/T	Radio Telephone
SAC	Superintendent Aircraft Construction
SAR	Search and Rescue
SCA	Superintending Captain of Aircraft
SL	Sea Lord (1/2SL – First/Second Sea Lord)
SNO	Senior Naval Officer
SS	Submarine Scout
SSE	Submarine Scout Experimental
SSP	Submarine Scout 'Pusher'
SSZ	Submarine Scout Zero
TSR	Torpedo, Spotter, Reconnaissance (after 1929)
WRNS	Women's Royal Naval Service

Ranks

Adm of the Fleet	
Adm	Admiral
VA	Vice-Admiral
RA	Rear-Admiral
Cdre	Commodore
Capt	Captain
Cdr	Commander
Lt-Cdr	Lieutenant-Commander
Lt	Lieutenant
Sub-Lt	Sub-Lieutenant
WO	Warrant Officer
FCPO	Fleet Chief Petty Officer
CPO	Chief Petty Officer
PO	Petty Officer
LM	Leading Mechanic
LS	Leading Seaman
AB	Able Seaman
AMI	Air Mechanic 1st Class
MRAF	Marshal of the Royal Air Force
ACM	Air Chief Marshal
AM	Air Marshal
AVM	Air Vice-Marshal
Air Cdre	Air Commodore
Gp Capt	Group Captain
Wg Cdr	Wing Commander

Acknowledgements

The author gratefully acknowledges the generous help given by his former colleagues in Director Public Relations (Navy) photographic section and in particular to Stuart Reed, Mike Gilbert who also did the last commission in HMS *Ark Royal*, Blondie Robertson, Alan Chadwick, John Anning and Lieutenant-Commander R. S. Bryden, MBE, DSC.

To Mike Farlam and Jim Baird (Westland Helicopters), Peter Bird and the late Tom Clarke (Vickers), Richard Catling (Rolls-Royce), Leading Airman (Photographer) D. J. Houghton, the Adastral House library staff for their unfailing help and courtesy, Ray Punnett, Jack White, and my editorial colleague and well-known author Bruce Robertson for his encouragement and loan of pictures from his extensive collection.

Finally, to my wife Eileen and son Anthony, to whom this book is dedicated.

11

LIGHTER THAN AIR

By 1907 the Royal Engineers and the Balloon Factory had perfected man-lifting kites, and Cody was firmly established as the Chief Kiting Instructor. Following a favourable report to Admiralty by Captain Osmond de Brock (Assistant Director Naval Intelligence) after a fact-finding mission to Farnborough, the Lords Commissioners sent the following letter to the Commander-in-Chief, HM Ships and Vessels, Portsmouth, dated 6 November 1907.

> Sir,
> I am commanded by my Lords Commissioners of the Admiralty to forward the attached copy of a report on the use of Cody's kites at Aldershot, and to direct that the Commanding Officer of HMS *Excellent* may be called upon to furnish his remarks as to the probable value of these kites for naval purposes.
>
> I am, Sir,
> Your obedient servant,
> C. I. Thomas (Secretary to the Admiralty)

Thus began the RN's second experiment with kites. Their Lordships were keen to ascertain their value when towed behind HM Ships and the trials were conducted by the CO of the Gunnery School, HMS *Excellent*, now Captain R. Tupper. With only short breaks at Farnborough where he was working on his aircraft, Cody was in HMS *Excellent* from 17 August to 7 October 1908, and the trials took place in HM ships *Grafton, Revenge, Fervent* and *Recruit*. The extrovert Cody astonished one ship's company by turning up on the jetty for sea trials, dressed in full cowboy gear including a 10-gallon stetson.

This is the right time to kill the myth, repeated by several writers, that it was the Navy's lack of kiting knowledge which led to the CO of HMS *Recruit* turning down wind on 31 August 1908, causing Cody to crash into the sea from 800 ft. It is difficult even to entertain this as fact when one remembers that officers and men had earlier trained at Farnborough where the kites were designed and made. What actually happened was that Cody was using an unusual combination of a pilot and four lifting kites, and the *Recruit*, steaming East in the Solent, ran out of the lee afforded by the Isle of Wight. A strong south wind hit the kiting array which went out of control. A smart piece of seamanship resulted in Cody, who was clinging to the basket, being picked up in a very short time by a ship's boat.

The Admiralty, now very interested in airships and aircraft, again wrote to C-in-C Portsmouth on 24 December:

Sir,
1. With reference to your letter of 22 October N3227/787/07, and later correspondence in regard to experiments with Cody's kites carried out by HMS *Excellent*, I am commanded by my Lords Commissioners of the Admiralty to acquaint you that, in view of the difficulties and risk at present attaching to the use of these kites, they consider it premature to supply them to sea-going ships, but HMS *Excellent* should be directed to keep in touch with any further developments in kites and kite flying.
2. I am to signify Their Lordships' directions to you to cause an expression of Their appreciation to be conveyed to the officers and men who conducted the experiments.

Their Lordships prepared to forget their brief experimental deviation and return to battleships, the solid and traditional weapon of the most powerful navy in the world, and airships.

The German Zeppelin LZ3 had made a maiden flight of 60 miles in 2 hours on 9 October 1906, and the civilian LZ4 had flown 200 miles in 12 hours on 1 July 1908.

Here in Britain as far back as 1903, the War Office had offered £4,000 for an airship capable of flying for 3 days with a crew of 3, and a speed of at least 16 knots.

Broadly speaking, the fabrics for making airship envelopes must have good gas-holding properties combined with mechanical strength and flexibility. Ideally, the gas loss should not exceed one per cent in 24 hours. Colonel J. L. B. Templer, when Commandant of the British Army Balloon Factory at Farnborough, had built for him two envelopes of goldbeaters' skin – made from the intestines of oxen. The first proved too heavy when inflated, but the second was satisfactory. During 1907, in an endeavour to provide themselves with an airship, the military authorities agreed to spend a further £2,000 on these experiments. Using the second envelope, a French-designed 50-hp engine, and a gondola and steering gear developed by Cody, Army Dirigible No. 1 was built at Farnborough. Named *Nulli Secundus*, she was 122 ft (37 m) long, had a diameter of 24 ft (8 m) and a capacity of 50,000 cft.

On Saturday 5 October with Colonel Capper (Templer's successor at Farnborough) as pilot and Cody as crew, the *Secundus* flew from

Farnborough to St Paul's, visiting on the way Trafalgar Square, Whitehall, Buckingham Palace, and eventually descended at Crystal Palace after a flight of 3 hours and 50 minutes and covering about 50 miles (80 kms). According to one newspaper report its appearance over the capital ". . . sent London wild with delight." The tiny 'blimp' does not appear to have been moored too securely and the following Thursday when high winds threatened to tear it free, the envelope was slit open to release the gas, and it became a mass of tangled wreckage. The remains were taken to Farnborough by road and later emerged as the framework for *Secundus 2*. She had, however, set up a British endurance record flight. *Secundus 2* only made a few trial flights locally at Farnborough, the last one on 15 August 1908, when its engine was found to be worn out.

On 23 October 1908, Prime Minister H. H. Asquith appointed a CID sub-committee to investigate 'Aerial Navigation', the rather peculiar name given to aviation generally. Their brief was to consider the advantages to be gained from airships or aeroplanes, and the amount of money to be allocated to various types of aerial experiments. Members of the committee included Rear-Admiral Sir C. L. Ottley, KCMG, CVO, and Captain R. H. S. Bacon (later Admiral Sir Reginald), DSO, CVO. Earlier, on 21 July, Bacon had submitted a paper to the First Sea Lord asking for the post of Naval Air Assistant to be created, liaison with the War Office, and the construction of a rigid airship. These draft proposals were accepted. In their report the committee referred to airships generally as being captive balloons, and to kites, dirigible balloons and aeroplanes. Captive balloons were seldom used by the Navy; kites were more valuable, especially in windy weather when captive balloons could not be used.

Although great progress had been made in the construction of dirigibles during the past year, the committee felt that the type for naval use needed rather special qualities: reliability, so it could operate away from base for several days; minimum leakage of gas; speed to make it independent of wind direction; reliable navigation instruments, and good wireless communications.

In their opinion the rigid frame would make secure moorings easier and the type would be used principally for scouting or spotting. At 1,000 ft on a clear day, the horizon could be seen for a distance of 40 miles, and at 2,000 ft, some 50 miles, as opposed to 12 miles from a ship. The cost of a rigid type was estimated to be £35,000, which compared favourably with £80,000 for a destroyer and £500,000 for a cruiser. The committee felt that the aeroplane was still in the experimental stage with the most successful of them (Wright Bros)

14

This picture emphasizes the origin of the aeroplane – a powered kite.

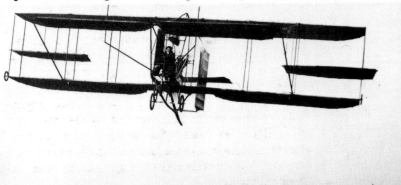

needing a launching aid, which was a disadvantage. In this country little progress had been made, except at South Farnborough where Cody had built one, and in Scotland where Lieutenant J. W. Dunne, RE, had built another. At present aeroplanes were of no practical value. There were, however, good grounds for believing that airships would be of great value of the Navy for scouting and bomb dropping, although these latter experiments were only in an early stage of development.

In their evidence to the sub-committee, both Navy members held firmly to the view that the captive balloon was not the best way for the Navy to obtain a wider field of view for scouting or spotting, and they came down heavily in favour of a rigid airship with fairly high speed and long range. Vickers Ltd were asked to tender for the rigid ship, and in their final report of 28 January 1909, the sub-committee recommended that a sum of £35,000 be included in the Naval Estimates for building it.

More importantly, despite the splendid work carried out by Dunne in Scotland and Cody at Farnborough, they recommended that experiments with aeroplanes at Military Ballooning Establishments be terminated and that the Services take advantage of private enterprise builders in this field. (Bearing this directive in mind it is difficult to see how the Navy came to be blamed at a later stage of the First World War, for 'cornering' the best brains in aviation. The difficult supply situation combined with inter-Service squabbles, were major factors in the decision to form the RAF.)

The committee also agreed that in the prevailing conditions, there was not much use in the Navy for aeroplanes, either for scouting or for operations over the sea.

The Cody Biplane, Army Aeroplane No. 1

The picture above and drawing below show Cody's aeroplane, built at an estimated cost of £1,000 and powered by two 50-hp engines. It was on 16 October 1908 that Cody made the first sustained flight at Farnborough Common (Hants) of 1,390 ft (423 m). The height was estimated at 30 ft (9 m) and the speed at between 25–30 mph (40–50 km/h or 22–28 knots). The aircraft had a wing span of 53 ft (16 m). Although this first flight ended in a crash with the left wings "crumpled up like tissue-paper" – in Cody's own words – the engine and propellers only sustained minor damage, and the main undercarriage was still capable of holding the machine up.

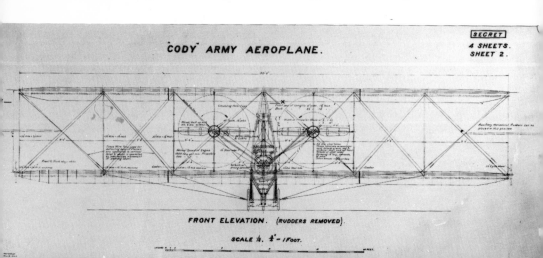

The 1909–1910 Naval Estimates included the sum of £35,000 for building Rigid Airship No. 1 (R1) and the Vickers estimate was accepted on 7 May 1909. The CID made the Navy responsible for the development of rigid airships and, originally, Captain Bacon was to have been responsible for seeing that the construction was according to the specifications drawn up. Bacon never took up the appointment, and in May a Special Air Department was set up to oversee the construction, with Captain Murray Sueter (later Rear-Admiral Sir Murray, MP) as the first Inspecting Captain of Airships (ICAS). The Air Branch included Commander Oliver Schwann (Assistant), and Lieutenants C. P. Talbot (Additional Assistant) and N. F. Usborne – later to lose his life when experimenting with launching aircraft from airships. Chief Artificer Sharpe completed the team who were borne on the books of HMS *Hermione*. One other man must be mentioned and he was Commander E. A. Masterman, whose pioneering work at Barrow-in-Furness during the construction of R1 led to the design of the Vickers-Masterman mooring mast.

During the period 20–23 May 1911, the R1 was moored to the mast in Cavendish Dock where a purpose-built shed had been constructed, and rode out gale force winds gusting to nearly 60 mph. Named *Mayfly*, to the amusement of its critics, the R1 never did. Mistakes are made in any new venture and she was at first overweight and lacked lift. After extensive modifications she became weakened structurally and later events were to prove Captain Sueter had been right when he disclaimed any responsibility for the design of R1, before accepting his appointment. While being manoeuvred out of its shed on 24 September 1911, the ship broke her back after being caught by a sudden gust of wind.

Shortly after this disaster, Sueter was sent to France, Austria and Germany, to have a look at airship developments. On his return, he was appointed the first Director of a yet unformed department at Admiralty – the Air Department – but retained his title as Inspecting Captain of Airships. His proposals for setting up a chain of Naval Air Stations around our coasts were accepted by the First Lord, Winston Churchill. *With characteristic foresight he noted that even though it might be necessary to win command of the air, it would involve the country in continuous and heavy expenditure!* A Zeppelin had overflown Sheerness and it was conceded that neither the base nor its warships had any defence to offer against it.

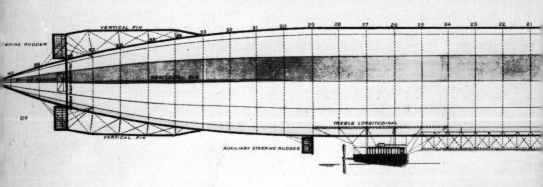

NAVAL AIRSHIP Nº I,

NAVAL AIRSHIP Nº I,

Sca

VERTICAL FIN

ERING RUDDER

33   32   31   30   29   28   27   26   25   24   23   22   21

HORIZONTAL FIN

D9

VERTICAL FIN

TREBLE LONGITUDINAL

AUXILIARY STEERING RUDDER

PARTICULARS OF RUDDERS, FINS &c.

DIVING RUDDERS:—

AREA OF THE TWO SETS ... 266 SQ. FEET.

TOTAL LIFT AT 3 LBS. PER SQ. FT. ... 798 LBS.

STEERING RUDDERS.

AREA OF THE TWO SETS ... 440 SQ. FEET.

TOTAL EFFORT AT 3 LBS. PER SQ. FT. 1320 LBS.

FINS

AREA OF HORIZONTAL FI

AREA OF VERTICAL FINS

AUXILIARY STEERING RUDDERS.

ONE SET. THREE PLANES ... TOTAL AREA ... 74 SQ. FEET.   MAX. EFFORT AT 3 LBS. PER SQ. FT. ... 222 LBS.

HM Naval Airship No. 1 (Rigid No. 1) is seen left floating in Cavendish Dock at Barrow-in-Furness. Below is a cutaway diagram of the airship taken from the original training manuals, as are the other airship diagrams in this section.

Commander E. A. D. Masterman has never officially been recognized for his pioneering work on the R1. He had qualified as a First Class Torpedo Lieutenant before being promoted to Commander at the early age of thirty, when he joined the small band of naval officers overseeing the building of the airship at Barrow. After a short spell at sea, he returned to aviation in September 1912, when posted to form and command the Naval Airship Section at Farnborough. After war broke out and the rigid airship programme got under way, Masterman became Trials Commander and was later promoted to Wing Captain. He formed a close working relationship with Barnes Wallis – earlier recruited by Vickers – during the building of R9 at Barrow. He later test-flew this airship. In September 1917, he was mainly responsible for an important policy document: 'The Uses of Airships in the Navy'.

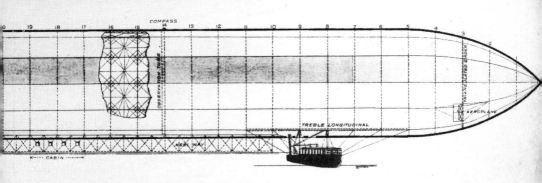

LAUNCHED, MAY 1911.

1' = 24 Feet.

On 3 January 1912 the Admiralty decided to close down airship construction and on the 25th, the Special Air Branch was disbanded.

Rear-Admiral E. C. T. Troubridge (later Admiral Sir Ernest) who was Chief of Staff, Admiralty, wrote a very important paper entitled 'Development of Naval Aeroplanes and Airships'. Dated 23 January, the paper proposed that a main aeroplane depot should be established just out of gun range from the sea, secure from raids by aeroplanes or airships, and suggested the defended port of Sheerness as a possible site, with sub-depots at main naval bases such as Tyne, Humber, Forth, and Harwich.

Admiral Troubridge went on to suggest that there was a need for a large twin-engined hydro-aeroplane (seaplane) for the rapid transport of passengers and urged that there should be 4–6 at each sub-depot, selected by a body under Captain Sueter, ICAS.

The paper proposed that a Volunteer Air Corps be formed for call-up in time of war, and that aeroplanes should be carried for trials in 4 large cruisers. On 1 July the Admiralty recommended the purchase of Willows No. 4 which was the first with fixed trimming blades at the tail end of the envelope. This small 'blimp' had a capacity of 20,000 cft, was 110 ft (33m) long with a two-man aluminium car. It went to the RN in October and was renumbered as HM Airship (HMA) No.2. By May 1914, it had been given a new envelope of goldbeaters' skin, the capacity had been increased to 35,000 cft, and it was later named Sea Scout (SS1).

Basically, there were three types of airship. The rigids had a frame covered by an envelope and remained the same shape when deflated. Within the frame was a series of gas-bags and the crew gondola was largely within the main structure.

The semi-rigids kept their shape by maintaining the internal pressure just above that of the atmosphere outside and had a rigid keel to which the gondola or crew cabin was attached.

The 'blimps' kept their shape in the same way as the semi-rigids but the gondola and engines were suspended from the envelope. All the earlier designs were of the 'blimp' type.

Captain Sueter was not the type to give in easily and although the Special Air Branch had been disbanded, he fought on, hoping to capitalize on the pioneering work done by Lieutenant Neville Usborne, who is generally credited with effectively solving the recovery of water from combustion gases, to counterbalance the weight of fuel burnt. This did much to reduce gas and ballast wastage. Finally, Sueter obtained permission from the Admiralty to place an order with Airships Limited, a firm owned by Mr Holt Thomas, for an Astra-

Torres non-rigid of 230,000 cft, a type which had proved very successful with the French Forces.

Shortly afterwards, he also obtained permission to buy a German non-rigid Parseval of 300,000 cft, which had two 170-hp engines and a speed of 46 mph. Ironically, when war broke out, the Parseval was one of the airships given the job of escorting the BEF to France.

The Astra-Torres became Naval Airship No. 3 and was the only British airship of the period to be armed, with a Hotchkiss machine-gun. The Parseval became No.4 and was later joined by 5, 6, and 7, all built under licence by Vickers Ltd. The first two were the only ones used operationally by the RNAS, Nos 5, 6 and 7 being used solely for training.

The committee also stated that the Naval Flying School at Eastchurch be responsible for elementary flying training and, after the establishment of CFS, should be used for experimental work and the specialist training of selected personnel. They stated it would be impossible to forecast any future use of aircraft in the Navy until experiments had been completed with take-off and landing on board ships, and hydroplanes had been developed sufficiently. Eastchurch was then under HMS *Actaeon* (Captain Paine) and all its personnel were on the books of the *Actaeon*.

On 7 May 1912, the same Technical Committee met to decide on the future provisions of airships for the RFC and again Sueter was a committee member. They came to the conclusion that airships were superior to aeroplanes for naval use in prolonged operations over the sea: that they had a greater radius of action; were better for wireless telegraphy; could carry a greater weight of explosives; and, because they could hover over a target, would be more accurate in a bombing attack. Airships had better and more stable platforms for photography and accurate observations. On 25 May it was recommended that a surplus Willows type be purchased for £1,050 and a Gamma type be built at the Royal Aircraft Factory for training naval personnel, at a cost of £5,000.

The Committee urged development of a small single-seater aeroplane which could be stowed easily for work with the Fleet and added that the formation of a branch so important as aeronautics could not be efficiently developed as a branch of the Torpedo School, as was now the case at Sheerness.

Private assistance was of importance, but the Navy should not rely too heavily on any one firm or the Royal Aero Club for assistance. *Shorts, the Admiral added, had not so far achieved anything of importance in the aeronautical world.*

On 27 February 1912 the Technical Committee of the CID recommended the setting up of a Royal Flying Corps with Naval and Military Wings. The German threat became more obvious in May when it was reported that the LZ3 military Zeppelin had flown nearly 400 miles at just over 40 knots, and had a lifting capacity of 7 tons, of which 3 could be explosives. On 13 April, the RFC was instituted and on the 23rd, the formation of the Central Flying School (CFS) was authorized by a Special Army Order, on 2,400 acres of land at Upavon Captain Godfrey Paine, MVO, (later Rear-Admiral Sir Godfrey and Commodore RNAS Training Establishment, Cranwell), was named as its first Commandant.

On 1 July it also became known that the first crews of the German Naval Airship Division had begun training at Nordholz near Cuxhaven. The same month, the Admiralty accepted a report asking for aeroplane stations at Dover, Sheppey (Eastchurch), Harwich Cromer, Cleethorpes, Filey, Newcastle, Rosyth, Aberdeen, Cromarty, Portsmouth, Plymouth, Weymouth and Pembroke; with airship stations at Chatham, the Norfolk Broads, and Rosyth.

On 25 September 1912, the Naval Airship Section was reconstituted at Farnborough under Commander E. A. Masterman who had earlier worked on the 'Mayfly' project (later Air Commodore, CB, CMB, CBE, AFC, and first Commandant, Royal Observer Corps). The other officers were Lieutenants N. F. Usborne, F. L. M. Boothby, and H. L. Woodcock, all of whom were attached to No. 1 Airship Squadron, Military Wing, under Major E. M. Maitland, to gain experience.

On 10 October the Admiralty approved a chain of Naval Air Stations round our coasts and provisions were made in the 1913–1914 Estimates for eight. This also appears to be the first time that a Naval Aviation Service was referred to in draft Naval Estimates. Before this, the embryo RNAS had been referred to as the Military Branch Royal Navy, and a seniority list gave: Sueter, Paine, Schwann (later Anglicized to Swann in May 1917, and Air Vice-Marshal Sir Oliver), Masterman, F. R. Scarlett (later Air Vice-Marshal), Maitland, Samson, Usborne, Longmore (later ACM Sir Arthur).

In November 1912, the Air Department was formed at Admiralty with Captain Sueter as the first Director Air Department (DAD). His assistants were Commander Swann, Lieutenant L'Estrange Malone and Engineer Lieutenant G. W. Caldwell.

In December 1913 it was stated that the primary role of the Naval Wing was reconnaissance, searching for enemy submarines and minefields, and spotting for guns. The strength was given as 8 biplanes, 5 monoplanes, 3 seaplanes, and Naval Airship No 2.

Intelligence sources suggested in February 1913 that the Germans had 12 airships and some bizarre suggestions were put forward for bringing them down. One in particular called for the construction of a special aircraft to overfly the Zeppelins and tear open their envelopes by means of steel hooks supported on hanging cables.

In June 1913 the Admiralty voted funds for 2 rigid and 6 non-rigid airships, and funding for the Naval Wing had risen from the modest £50,000 of 1911 to £321,000 for 1913. On 10 July the Admiralty announced the historic Fleet manoeuvres in which 351 ships took part and aircraft operated with the Fleet for the first time.

Meanwhile, the Navy had taken over the largest shed at Farnborough, 'A' shed, and Commander Masterman who had qualified as a pilot in *Beta* took over the four airships – *Beta*, *Delta*, *Gamma* and *Eta* – when the Army Airship Section was disbanded on 1 January 1914. The Administration of the Naval Wing was under Captain C. F. Lambert (later Admiral Sir Cecil) the Fourth Sea Lord, and on 8 January he convened a meeting at Admiralty of senior air personnel, to consider the final organization of the Royal Naval Air Service. On 17 March, Churchill told a packed House that the RNAS had 103 aircraft of which 62 were seaplanes. There were 120 regular pilots of whom 20 held Royal Aero Club certificates, 1 petty officer pilot, and 540 men.

With the take-over of the Army airships, Major Maitland became second-in-command to Masterman, and after the Royal Naval Air Service officially came into being on 1 July 1914, they both organized the mobilization of the Airship Section for the Fleet Review at Spithead between 18–22 July. Masterman flew over the Fleet in the former *Delta*. The RNAS as a separate entity consisted of the Admiralty Air Department; Central Air Office, Sheerness; RN Flying School, Eastchurch, and the Naval Air Stations. New ranks introduced were: Wing Captain (Captain RN), Wing Commander (Commander RN), Squadron Commander (Lieutenant-Commander RN), Flight-Commander or Flight-Lieutenant (Lieutenant RN), and Flight Sub-Lieutenant (Sub-Lieutenant RN).

Lord Fisher, the First Sea Lord, held a meeting at Admiralty on 31 October 1914, which was attended by Holt Thomas. Fisher was satisfied that the small airship would be of great value in anti-submarine detection, an idea pushed by Thomas in a series of letters. The first type ordered was the well-proven Willows No. 4. Squadron Commander Usborne took over all development work on airship envelopes and Squadron Commander E. F. Briggs, the work on engines. On 28 February 1915, Masterman was put in charge of the Airship Section of the Air Department and he later became Wing Captain in charge of trials for the rigid programme. His first job was to invite firms to tender for a Submarine Scouting airship, the SS type. The RNAS eventually produced the first SS No. 1 themselves by using an old Willows envelope and a BE2c fuselage.

The first SS Base was established at Capel, Folkestone, on 8 May 1915, and the second at Polegate, Eastbourne, on 6 July. The Willows SS2 was delivered to Kingsnorth in March. The average dimensions were: length 143 ft (44m), overall height 43 ft (13m), maximum diameter (central section) 28 ft (8m), and capacity 60,000 cft. The car was a BE2c aeroplane body less the wings, rudder and elevators, with a 75-hp Renault engine driving a 9-ft diameter four-bladed propeller. Maximum speed at 1,600 ft (488m) was 46 mph and the estimated endurance was then 8 hours. Net lift (armament, two crew and fuel) was 1,434 lb (652 kg). The later types with an Armstrong Whitworth car were similar, but had a 100-hp Green engine rigged to a 70,000 cft envelope. At 1,150 revolutions a minute, they averaged 49 mph and climbed at 500 ft a minute. Net lift was 1,700 lb (772 kg) of which about 470 lb (214 kg) could be bombs. Both cars were tractor types. The improved SS had an endurance of 12 hours at full speed.

GENERAL ARRANGEMENT OF "S.S." AIRSHIP.
A.W. TYPE.

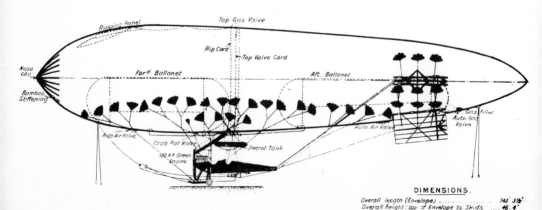

DIMENSIONS.

Overall length (Envelope) .... 143' 3½'
Overall height (top of Envelope to Skids .... 46. 4'
Maximum diameter (Envelope ... . 30'

VOLUME OF ENVELOPE. 70,000 CU FT. BALLONETS 9,800 CU FT EACH

ARRANGEMENT OF S.S. AIRSHIP.

Z. TYPE.

SCALE 1/200

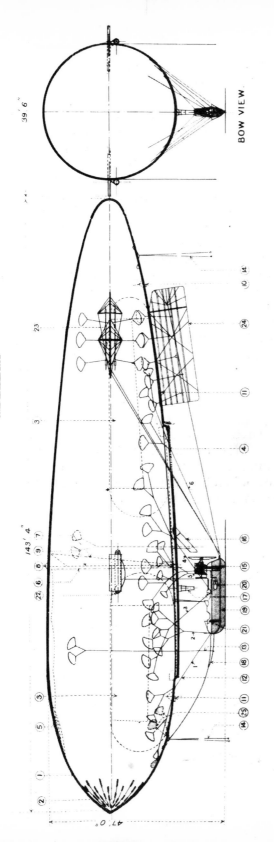

BOW VIEW.

39' 6"

143' 4"

47' 0"

DESCRIPTION

Nº		Nº	
1	Envelope	13	Midship Handling Guys
2	Nose Stiffeners	14	Handling Guys
3	Ballonets	15	Engine
4	Crabpots	16	Blower Pipe.
5	Ripping Panel	17	Auxily Blower Pipe.
6	Ripping Cord	18	Trail & Grapnel Rope
7	Tricing Line	19	Car.
8	Top Gas Valve	20	Bomb.
9	Top Valve Cord	21	Lewis Gun.
10	Bottom Gas Valve	22	Petrol Tank.
11	Auto Air Valve	23	Horizontal & Elevator Planes.
12	Suspension.	24	Vertical & Rudder Plane.
		25	Strengthening of Fore anchoring point for Mooring-Out.

PARTICULARS

Capacity of Envelope	70.000 Cu. Ft.
" " Ballonets	9800 Cu. Ft. each.
Overall Length of Envelope	143' 4"
" Height (ground to top of envelope)	47' 0"
" Width	39' 6"
Maximum Speed	53 M. P. H.
Engines (H. P. & number of)	1-75 H.P. Rolls-Royce.
Armament	1 Lewis Gun, 2-65 Lb. Bombs.
Crew	3

By the end of the year 1916, 50 SS ships had been completed and all of them did excellent work. Admiralty approval was given in January 1916 for 6 SSP ships, but later the same year an experimental SS Zero was built at Folkestone and proved so successful it was decided to adopt the type as the standard Submarine Scout.

On 7 April 1917, approval was given to build 16 SSZ ships with a boat-shaped car having seating for three – pilot, wireless rating and engineer – rigged to a 70,000-cft envelope with a 75-hp Rolls-Royce Hawk engine. The last of the 16 was delivered on 24 July and they all proved very satisfactory with speeds of up to 50 mph. At the end of the year there were 18 in commission. Three had been lost at sea, and 2 each were supplied to the American and French governments.

Construction of the Coastal type of airship (below) was completed by the end of 1916 when 32 had been built, with 4 being sold to the Russians and 1 to the French. At the end of 1917 only 13 remained in commission and 3 were being rebuilt. Nine had been lost during operations. The Coastals were replaced by the North Sea Star type with a capacity of 210,000 cft compared with the 170,000 cft of the Coastals.

There were 17 of the even bigger North Sea type built, the first completing her trials on 1 February 1917. They were the last of the non-rigids to be built for the Navy. The envelope was a streamlined Astra of 360,000 cft rigged to a car made of wood covered with duralumin sheets. Originally they had 2 Rolls-Royce engines of 250-hp each, which were carried in a separate power unit set on gantries at the end of a gangway from the car. Most of the rigging was internal, therefore the car was closer to the envelope and speeds of 44 mph were common at only 1,250 rpm. This gave an endurance of about 24 hours. These ships set up some remarkable endurance flights with NS1 flying 1,500 miles in 49 hours 22 minutes in 1917. In 1919, NS11 flew 4,000 miles in 101 hours to set up an endurance record for non-rigids.

GENERAL ARRANGEMENT OF COASTAL AIRSHIP

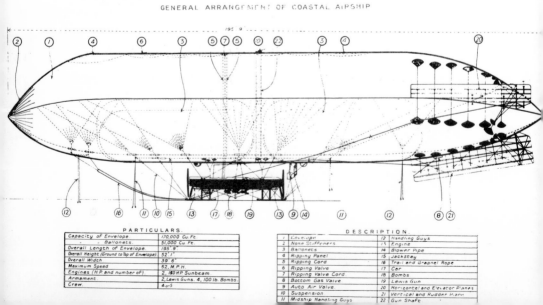

PARTICULARS.	
Capacity of Envelope	170,000 Cu.Ft.
Ballonets	51,000 Cu.Ft.
Overall Length of Envelope	195'9"
Overall Height (Ground to Top of Envelope)	52'1"
Overall Width	39'6"
Maximum Speed	52, M.P.H.
Engines (H.P. and number of)	2, 150 H.P. Sunbeam.
Armament	2, Lewis Guns. 4, 100 lb. Bombs.
Crew.	4 or 5

DESCRIPTION.			
1	Envelope	12	Handling Guys
2	Nose Stiffeners	13	Engine
3	Ballonets	14	Blower Pipe
4	Ripping Panel	15	Jackstay
5	Ripping Cord	16	Trail and Grapnel Rope
6	Ripping Valve	17	Car
7	Ripping Valve Cord.	18	Bombs
8	Bottom Gas Valve	19	Lewis Gun
9	Auto Air Valve	20	Horizontal and Elevator Planes
10	Suspension	21	Vertical and Rudder Planes
11	Midship Handling Guys	22	Gun Shaft

The first rigid airship, HMA R9, incorporated the lessons learned from the R1 failure and there were several interesting modifications. The transverse section of the ship was a 17-sided polygon instead of 12 as in No. 1, and envelope capacity had been increased from 663,518 cft to 889,310 cft.

As originally planned, R9 was to have four 6-cylinder Wolseley Maybach engines, two in each of the two gondolas. There was an accommodation cabin for the crew and a W/T office, towards the rear of the ship.

Built by Vickers at Barrow, the R9 was found to have a serious deficiency in lift during the first trials of 16 November 1916. To lighten the ship as much as possible, the crew accommodation was dispensed with and only the small wireless cabin retained. At the same time, the two engines were removed from the after-gondola together with the transmission gear to the swivelling propellers. These were replaced by a single 250-hp Maybach engine from the Zeppelin L33 which had been forced down and captured in Essex on 24 September 1916. This single engine had direct transmission to a single 2-bladed propeller 17 ft (5 m) in diameter. The two forward engines drove 4-bladed swivelling propellers which were 12 ft (3.6 m) in diameter.

The total length was 520 ft (159 m) with a hull diameter of 53 ft (16 m), and overall height of 72 ft (22 m). The hull was divided into 17 compartments each 40 ft (9 m) long, containing one gas-bag each. These were replaced too with new ones of single-ply cotton fabric, rubber-proofed on one face, with two instead of three layers of goldbeaters' skin to reduce permeability.

The hauling-down rope forward was a Manilla hemp 3½ inches in diameter, 300 ft (91 m) long with a breaking strain of 7.5 tons (7.6 tonnes). The sea-anchor and hauling-down wire rope was 1¼ inches in diameter, 300 ft long, with the same breaking strain.

The wireless cabin housed a Marconi 30-watt Type 56 transmitter with a range of 350-400 miles and a Tc receiver with a 3-valve amplifier, suitable for receiving spark signals up to a wavelength of 600 metres. The 300-ft trailing aerial was let out through a duralumin tube in the floor of the cabin.

The gondolas were originally fitted with two swivelling landing wheels on each, but they gave continuous trouble from the start and were replaced with a Palmer cord bumping bag. Beneath the decking of each car were 16 buoyancy bags in case of a sea landing. There were walkways at the top of the hull to reach gun platforms and along the keel, to connect the gondolas and wireless cabin.

R9 did her next trial flight over Morecambe Bay on 27 November

H.M. RIGID AIRSHIP No. 9.

ELEVATION, PLAN, BOW AND STERN VIEWS OF SHIP.

Gun Platform for two Lewis guns

Station for one Lewis gun

Length of Hull 520 ft.

Fore Car
Main Control Position
Two engines each 180 H.P.
Swivelling propellers

Officer's Cabin
Crews Quarters

After Car
Auxy Control Position
One engine 240 H.P.
Fixed propeller.

Length overall 526' 0"

ELEVATION.

PARTICULARS

Length overall 526 ft.
Extreme width 53 ft
Extreme height 76 ft 6 ins

Total lift at 95% full = 845,540 cu.ft = 256 tons.

Armament Three Lewis guns

Total horse-power 600
Estimated speed 45 M.P.H.

Max. height 76·6

BOW VIEW

Max. Diam. of Hull 53·0"

STERN VIEW

External Corridor   From Ring 2 to   Ring 17

VIEW FROM UNDERNEATH

1917, and then did two speed trials on 13 December, averaging 41.8 mph (36 knots). The modifications already described started on 5 January 1917 and were completed on 17 March. The final trial flight was on 23 March and she left for Howden on 4 April.

On 21 July, R9 set up a British record endurance flight for a rigid airship when she covered 430 miles in 26¾ hours. She was to prove invaluable for training crews and escort duties over the east coast.

On the original trials the crew and passengers were: Wing Captain E. A. Masterman, pilot; Squadron Commander T. K. Elmsley, assistant pilot; Engineer Lt-Cdr G. Villar; Messrs H. Pratt and J. Watson (Messrs Vickers); WO2s Messrs B. S. Brice and A. Bushfield; CPOs Simmons, Matthews, Coward, Miller, Mathewson and Cook; PO Robinson; LM Smith and AM1 Turley.

The Admiralty's aim to have a fleet of rigid airships led to the ordering on 16 October 1915 and 6 January 1916, of the four ships of the R23 Class. These followed the main design features of R9 but the envelope capacity was increased to 997,500 cft; length to 535 ft (163 m); gas-bags and compartments to 18, and they had a crew of 16 plus 2 supernumeraries.

Nos 23 and 26 were built by Vickers at Barrow; No. 24 by William Beardmore at Ichinnan, Renfrewshire; and No. 25 by Armstrong Whitworth at Barlow. The engine arrangements were different. The centre engine housing carried two 250-hp Rolls-Royce engines driving single fixed propellers, and the fore and aft gondolas had a single 250-hp engine driving swivelling propellers mounted on either side of their respective cars. Two parachutes were fitted in No. 23 for experimental purposes.

The main transmitter was a Type 56A, the Cranwell modification of the De Forrest Oscillion with a range of 600 miles, and a power of 150 watts. The original Td for receiving continuous wave or spark signals was to be replaced by a new Tf, enabling airships to communicate with each other or their base, with minimum interference. The main transmitter was powered by ten 72-cell Ediswan dry batteries in series.

A 2-pounder gun was to have been mounted but again, insufficient lift in the class led to modifications to save weight and although gun trials were carried out at Pulham, it was considered the rate of fire was insufficient and hull damage might result. The bomb frames were removed together with the gun and five Lewis guns substituted.

On speed trials No. 23 averaged 51.7 mph (45 knots) at Pulham on 13 November 1917, and the others were delivered after their first flights: No. 24 on 28 October 1917; No. 25 on 14 October 1917, and No. 26 on 22 April 1918.

Four improved 23X Class were ordered but two, Nos 28 and 30, were cancelled following the capture of the German Zeppelin L33.

The last of the rigids were powered by five 250-hp Rolls-Royce engines. No. 31 had a capacity of 1,500,000 cft, while Nos 33 and 34 – based on the design of the captured Zeppelin – had a capacity of 2,000,000 cft. In July 1919, R34 made the air return crossing of the Atlantic from East Fortune, Scotland, to Long Island, USA. She took 108 hours 12 minutes to cover the 3,130 miles.

On 1 January 1918, the Airship Section of the RNAS had expanded to a total of 382 officers and 5,457 men, operating from 15 flying stations at home and 1 abroad. There were 8 construction stations. During 1917, they flew a total of 21,699 hours.

A few other points are worthy of note in this brief summary. After preliminary training, which naval pilots did in a 'free balloon' either at Kingsnorth or Wormwood Scrubs, they usually went solo after a month. This was followed by a course in navigation in HMS *Vernon* and one in gunnery in HMS *Excellent*. There was also an introductory course in engineering in HMS *Fisgard*. Then the student pilot started his course in airship flying and undertook his first solo flight after 4 hours' instruction. The 'graduate' examination consisted of papers on armament, engineering, meteorology and aerostatics, with practical work on rigging and signalling. On successful completion of the course, the pilot was posted to an operational unit.

It speaks highly for the instructors and the quality of the men, that although nearly 400 airships were built and flew over 2½ million miles, only 46 officers and men lost their lives. Several of these were in ships destined to meet enemy aircraft against which they stood little chance, such as the C17 shot down on 21 April 1917, and the C27 shot down on 11 December of the same year.

On a happier note, the last of the Coastal types flew from Kingsnorth to Pulham where Colonel Maitland (the ex-Farnborough Army officer who transferred to the RNAS) was Commanding Officer. On 13 February 1917, the Colonel made what is believed to be the first live parachute drop from an airship from 1,000 ft (305 m) and landed safely.

Finally, one of the most momentous flights of the war was undoubtedly that completed by Captain G. M. Meager, with Captain T. B. Williams, AFC, as second pilot, on 28 October 1918. They flew the Italian built SR1 (441,000 cft) from Ciampino, Italy, to RNAS Kingsnorth, in 3½ days. This was the biggest non-rigid airship ever in naval service and the achievement gained Meager a well-deserved AFC and the Italian *Croix de Guerre*.

32

AIRSHIPS IN COMMISSION
Officially reported 17 October 1918

Anglesey Naval Airship Station (sub-station at Maiahide)

Number	Type	Engine
31	SSZ	75-hp R.R.
33	SSZ	75-hp R.R.
34	SSZ	75-hp R.R.
35	SSZ	75-hp R.R.
50	SSZ	75-hp R.R.

Cranwell Naval Airship Station (School)

25	Rigid	4 R.R. Eagle 3
1	SSP	110-hp Berliet
5	SSP	110-hp Berliet
6	SSP	110-hp Berliet
28a	SS (M.F.)	75-hp R.R.
29	SS (M.F.)	75-hp R.R.
30a	SS (M.F.)	75-hp R.R.
31a	SS (M.F.)	75-hp R.R.
37a	SS (M.F.)	110-hp Berliet
39a	SS (M.F.)	110-hp Berliet
9	SST	2 75-hp R.R.
61	SSZ	75-hp R.R.

East Fortune (sub-station at Chathill)

1	C Star	1 110-hp Berliet
		1 240-hp Renault
3	C Star	1 110-hp Berliet
		1 240-hp Fiat
8	C Star	1 110-hp Berliet
		1 240-hp Fiat
7	NS	2 240-hp Fiat
8	NS	2 240-hp Fiat
29	Rigid	4 275-hp R.R.
3	SSZ	75-hp R.R.
59	SSZ	75-hp R.R.
60	SSZ	75-hp R.R.

Folkestone (sub-station at Godmersham Park)

1	SST	2 75-hp R.R.
8	SST	2 75-hp R.R.
1	SSZ	75-hp R.R.
4	SSZ	75-hp R.R.
18	SSZ	75-hp R.R.
29	SSZ	75-hp R.R.
36	SSZ	75-hp R.R.
46	SSZ	75-hp R.R.
69	SSZ	75-hp R.R.

Howden (sub-stations at Lowthorpe and Kirkleatham)

2	C Star	1 110-hp Berliet
		1 240-hp Fiat
4	C Star	1 110-hp Berliet
		1 240-hp Fiat
9	C Star	1 110-hp Berliet
		1 240-hp Fiat
6	Parseval	2 220-hp Renault
3	SST	2 75-hp R.R.
4	SST	2 75-hp R.R.
5	SST	2 75-hp R.R.
7	SST	2 75-hp R.R.
32	SSZ	75-hp R.R.
55	SSZ	75-hp R.R.

62	SSZ	75-hp R.R.
63	SSZ	75-hp R.R.
64	SSZ	75-hp R.R.

Larne (caretaker) for Longside (sub-station at Auldba

4	Coastal	1 110-hp Berliet
		1 220-hp Renault
5	C Star	1 110-hp Berliet
		1 240-hp Fiat
7	C Star	1 110-hp Berliet
		1 240-hp Fiat
5a	Coastal	1 160-hp Sunbeam
		1 220-hp Renault
6	NS	2 240-hp Fiat
9	NS	2 240-hp Fiat
10	NS	2 240-hp Fiat
11	NS	2 240-hp Fiat
57	SSZ	75-hp R.R.
58	SSZ	75-hp R.R.
65	SSZ	75-hp R.R.
66	SSZ	75-hp R.R.

Luce Bay

11	SSZ	75-hp R.R.
12	SSZ	75-hp R.R.
20	SSZ	75-hp R.R.

Mullion (sub-stations at Toller, Laira, Bude)

6	C Star	1 110-hp Berliet
		1 240-hp Fiat
10	C Star	1 110-hp Berliet
		1 240-hp Fiat
2	Coastal	1 110-hp Berliet
		1 220-hp Renault
14	SSZ	75-hp R.R.
27	SSZ	75-hp R.R.
40	SSZ	75-hp R.R.
42	SSZ	75-hp R.R.
45	SSZ	75-hp R.R.
47	SSZ	75-hp R.R.

Pembroke (sub-station at Wexford)

16	SSZ	75-hp R.R.
37	SSZ	75-hp R.R.
52	SSZ	75-hp R.R.
53	SSZ	75-hp R.R.
56	SSZ	75-hp R.R.
56	SSZ	75-hp R.R.

Polegate (sub-stations at Slindon, Upton)

6	SSZ	75-hp R.R.
8	SSZ	75-hp R.R.
9	SSZ	75-hp R.R.
19	SSZ	75-hp R.R.
28	SSZ	75-hp R.R.
30	SSZ	75-hp R.R.
39	SSZ	75-hp R.R.
41	SSZ	75-hp R.R.
43	SSZ	75-hp R.R.
44	SSZ	75-hp R.R.
45	SSZ	75-hp R.R.

Pulham (Experimental)

14a	Coastal	1 110-hp Berliet
		1 220-hp Renault
23	Rigid	3 R.R. Eagle 3
		1 R.R. Eagle 6
24	Rigid	4 R.R. Eagle 3
26	Rigid	4 275-hp R.R.
14a	SS	75-hp R.R.
35	SS	75-hp R.R.
36	SS	75-hp Renault
2	SSE	2 75-hp R.R.

AIRSHIPS UNDER CONSTRUCTION

Number	Type	Builders	Engine
31	Rigid	Short, Bedford	5 275-hp R.R.
32	Rigid	Short, Bedford	5 275-hp R.R.
33	Rigid	Armstrong, Barlow	5 270-hp Sunbeam
34	Rigid	Beardmore, Inchinnan	6 270-hp Sunbeam
35	Rigid	Armstrong, Barlow	4 350-hp Sunbeam
36	Rigid	Beardmore, Inchinnan	4 350-hp Sunbeam
37	Rigid	Short, Bedford	4 350-hp Sunbeam
80	Rigid	Vickers, Barrow	4 250-hp Wolseley-Maybach

6 NS Type with 2 × 300-hp Fiat engines were being built at Kingsnorth, Nos 12, 13, 14, 15, 16, 17.

2 SSZ Types built at Wormwood Scrubs with single 75-hp R.R. engines had been shipped to Kassandra on 24 August 1918, Nos 68, 70.

106 SS Twin Types numbered from 10–115 were being built at Wormwood Scrubs and Kingsnorth with varying engines: Nos 10–12 with 2 × 75-hp R.R. engines; 13–29 with 2 × 110-hp Berliet engines; Nos 30–68 with R.R. engines – all being built at Wormwood Scrubs. Nos 69–90 with Berliet engines; Nos 91–115 with R.R. engines – were being built at Kingsnorth.

In addition Kingsnorth had NS No. 4 with 2 × 240-hp Fiat engines and SSE 3 with 2 × 75-hp R.R. engines on trials, and SST 2 with 2 × 75-hp R.R. engines was being repaired.

Summary for 1917–1918 as of 1 January 1918

Station	Hours Flown	Officers	Men
Anglesey	1,570	18	157
Barrow	20	20	340
Caldale	340	6	85
Cranwell	781	47	203
East Fortune	2,100	32	580
Folkestone	1,904	19	247
Howden	2,086	40	612
Kingsnorth	211	38	755
Longside	1,250	25	520
Luce Bay	1,765	13	155
Mullion	2,845	25	362
Pembroke	2,152	22	281
Polegate	2,800	37	264
Pulham	1,840	29	651
Wormwood Scrubs	35	11	245
Totals	21,699	382	5,457

There were 15 Airship Stations in commission of which 11 were active. Of the remaining 4, Cranwell had been largely developed during 1917 as a Training Establishment, with Barrow, Kingsnorth and Wormwood Scrubs becoming constructional.

Construction Shed	Purpose
Barking	Stores and experiments
Barlow	Rigid, Armstrong Whitworth
Barrow	Rigid, Vickers
Bedford	Rigid, Shorts
Flookburgh	Vickers (now abandoned)
Inchinnan	Rigid, Beardmore
Kingsnorth	Rigid construction station
Wormwood Scrubs	SS construction station

Airship State: There were 68 in commission and 27 out of action. R9, R23, R24, and R25 had been accepted and the hull of 26 completed.

Of the 23X Class, the hulls of 29 and 30 were nearly complete with 28 and 30 being abandoned. Considerable progress had been made with 31 and 32 of the modified Schutte-Lanz type.

Approval was given for the construction of 16 ships of the R33 Class. Five were building with R33 and R34 being assembled.

On 16 August 1917, it was reported that a pigeon service had commenced between Pulham and Felixstowe. Out of 566 sent for training purposes, 544 arrived.

At Wormwood Scrubs, 833 balloon trips were made by day and 35 by night with a total of 3,645 officers and men making ascents, and 172 qualified as pilots.

A BRIGHT BEGINNING

"We have acquired some land at Eastchurch for flying purposes. The buildings and sheds for the Naval Aviation School are in course of erection. A considerable number of aeroplanes have been purchased both for training and experimental purposes, principally in England, and some of them are being adapted for the special needs of the Navy . . ."

When Winston Churchill, First Lord of the Admiralty wrote these words in an explanatory statement to the 1912 Naval Estimates, he made it clear to the world that the Royal Navy was taking heavier-than-air machines seriously. The date was 18 March 1912.

The Navy had not always taken aeroplanes so seriously. As far back as 1907, the Wright Brothers – who had made a flight of 25 miles (40 kms) in October 1905 – had offered to sell their patents to the Admiralty but it was refused because, in the opinion of the Admiralty, "they will not be of any practical use to the Naval Service". With few exceptions, Senior NOs continued to turn a convenient 'blind eye' to what was happening in the aeronautical field at home and abroad. In their specifications for a flying machine the War Office had stated categorically: ". . . on all trials the machine must rise from the ground under its own power without special starting devices." This ruled out the Wright aeroplane.

In many ways 1908 was perhaps the most exciting year for aviation generally. On 12 September, the Wrights flew 50 miles (80 kms), and on 16 October, Cody made the first sustained flight in Great Britain when he flew 1,390 ft (423 m) on Farnborough Common. On 5 November at Blair Atholl, Scotland, the other great pioneer Dunne, had flown a distance of 40 yards. The international interest in aviation reached such proportions that the Navy sent Captain R. H. Bacon, RN, to France, to report on the air races at Rheims. Prior to this, the Navy was firmly of the opinion that lighter-than-air machines were the answer to the Navy's special needs because of the airship's greater load-carrying capacity, its range, and its ability to adjust its speed to that of the Fleet with which it was working. When Captain Bacon returned from France, however, fired with enthusiasm for the new 'flying machines', he advised that a Special Air Department be set up, that the post of Naval Air Assistant be created, and that there should be more liaison with the War Office and the building of the rigid airship *Mayfly*. There were further important developments in 1909 beginning in January when Commander R. A. Newton wrote the first published work on aerial navigation. On 25 July, Louis Bleriot won the *Daily Mail* prize for the first cross-Channel flight from Calais–Dover, with a time of 37 minutes.

By the end of 1910, it was estimated that the French had 32 aircraft of various types. Early in 1912, they had 234 war planes and the Military/ Naval Air Estimates were £950,000. In addition, 300 aircraft were on order and there were 300 flying officers licensed by the French Aero Club. We were a long way behind despite the active lobbying by a dedicated band of NOs to encourage official interest in aeroplanes. The very first naval pilot was Lieutenant G. C. Colmore who qualified at his own expense and was awarded Aviator's Certificate No. 15, on 21 June 1910.

In April 1911 when the Air Battalion was first formed with a flying school at Netheravon on Salisbury Plain, we had six qualified pilots. For the year ending 31 March 1912, only £113,000 was spent on aviation and this included £28,000 for the new airship shed at Farnborough. The school at Netheravon was geared for three terms of four months each, with a through-put of 180 officers a year. After successfully completing their final examinations, the pilots could reclaim the £75 it had cost them to learn to fly privately, and could choose between naval or military flying. Alternatively, they could go to a Reserve which was of two kinds. The first category received a retaining fee for completing a few cross-country flights each year; the second category was only available in time of war.

In fact, Messrs Vickers had told the Admiralty in January 1911, that they could build under licence a French aircraft able to take off from HM Ships only to have Admiralty reply that they were not proposing to buy any aircraft for the Royal Navy. Yet in December 1910, they had already succumbed to pressure from the Royal Aero Club which had purchased some land on a farm to provide flying facilities for members. It was adjacent to the factory of Short Brothers at Eastchurch. The Club now offered aircraft and tuition free to NOs who wanted to train as pilots. In response to a General Fleet Order issued by Admiralty, over 200 would-be pilots volunteered and from these 5 were selected – 3 from the RN and 2 from the Royal Marines.

One volunteer dropped out through illness, but the remaining four reported on 2 March 1911, to an odd assortment of huts and hangars on the eastern end of the Isle of Sheppey. The 'airfield' ran round the bottom of the hill in a gentle undulating slope. The first four were Lieutenants C. R. Samson, HMS *Foresight* – surely an appropriate name; A. M. Longmore, Torpedo Boat No 24; R. Gregory, HMS *Antrim*; and E. L. Gerrard, Royal Marine Light Infantry, from HMS

Hermione. The last man of the original selection, Lieutenant G. Wildman-Lushington, Royal Marine Artillery, joined them before completion of the joint flying and engineering course.

They were all trained by Mr Horace Short and Mr C. B. Cockburn, on various types of aircraft lent free by Mr F. McClean. Instruction was far from easy, with the pupil huddled up behind the instructor and getting the feel of the controls by reaching over his shoulder. With Cockburn weighing 196 lb (88 kg) and Gerrard only a little less, the Short Farman-type 'pushers' had a job even getting off the ground. Instruction usually took place at dawn, to take advantage of calm wind conditions. If the wind speed was over 10 knots no flying took place. In straight flight the height was often only 30 ft (9 m) and it was reported that some watchers lay flat on the ground to make sure the aircraft really left it.

Of the three original machines, Nos 26 and 34 were fitted with a 50-hp Gnome rotary and No. 28 was the first fitted with the 60-hp Green. Mr McClean also provided a variety of other aircraft: No. 9, a monoplane built by the Universal Aviation Company; No. 39, a Short biplane – the first twin-engined aircraft that ever flew; and a Short S27 with a 70-hp Gnome. The modified S27 with three pontoon-shaped flotation bags attached was to achieve everlasting fame on 1 December 1911, when Longmore (later ACM Sir Arthur) flew it from Eastchurch and landed on the River Medway – another first in the rapidly growing field of naval aviation.

The four aviators completed the first part of their training on 25 April 1911, with Samson obtaining Certificate No. 71, Longmore No. 72, and Lieutenant W. Parke (trained at Hendon) No. 73. The next to qualify were Gregory (No. 75) and Gerrard (No. 76), on 2 May. They were later joined by another naval aviator destined to become famous, Lieutenant Richard Bell Davies, who qualified at his own expense on 30 May, with Certificate No. 90.

It is interesting to note that on 1 July, the Gordon Bennett International Speed Race was won by a Frenchman flying a Nieuport monoplane, and Gerrard was sent to Pau to learn how to fly this type. Before he even began, however, the Admiralty and War Office banned monoplanes because of several fatal accidents. The naval pilots completed their mandatory 6 months' flying training on 1 September, after technical engineering instruction at Brooklands, attending the Military Trials at Rheims and visiting the principal aircraft works in France. They were borne on the books of HMS *Wildfire*.

In October, Samson persuaded the Admiralty to purchase two of the McClean machines and to detail 12 ratings to work at Eastchurch. The Admiralty also entered into an agreement with Shorts to purchase 10 acres of land from them near the RAC's aerodrome. The ratings were borne on the books of HMS *Actaeon*, and the tiny village of Eastchurch was rapidly becoming the centre of naval air activity, with hangars and accommodation being added to the sheds of the Royal Aero Club.

The Short S27 was the beginning of a continuing series of Short aircraft and led to the development of the first tractor biplane built by the Company (serial T5). It was used by the Navy as a landplane and as a seaplane, with one main float and two wing floats.

The first British take-off from water owed much to the determination and free-enterprise of Commander Oliver Schwann (later Swann), and his brother officers of the Naval Airship Tender HMS *Hermione*, who were working at Barrow on the construction of the *Mayfly* by Vickers. In March, the firm of A. V. Roe built the Avro Type D biplane with a 35-hp Green engine and on 11 April, Lieutenant W. Parke, RN, who had never been in the aeroplane before, flew it the length of the aerodrome and declared it stable, easy to fly and without vices. After a 'trial flight' in June, Commander Swann and brother officers purchased the aircraft for a reputed £750 and had it crated and sent to Barrow by rail. The wheels were removed and skids were fastened to types of 'floats' designed by Swann and brother officers, and built by naval personnel. These were modified after trials to the stepped type of float and on 18 November 1911, the unexpected happened. During taxying trials, the seaplane lifted off its step and reached a height of 20 ft (6 m). Swann was unqualified at the time and the aircraft crashed back into the water. (Swann was awarded Certificate 203, 16 April 1912.) The importance of Longmore's experiment in landing on water with flotation bags, and of Swann in taking off from water, was in the valuable contribution they made to the progress of naval aviation and the influence they had on many senior naval officers who had seen little practical value in naval aircraft before.

The last event of note in 1911 was the design of the first aerial compass (Pattern 200) by Captain Creagh-Osborne. Events now began to move with ever more exciting trials. Lieutenant Longmore and Mr Oswald Short were experimenting with flotation bags and Samson was at Chatham Dockyard building a trackway along the forecastle of the battleship HMS *Africa*. He modified a Short S27 biplane with three flotation bags and on 10 January, Lieutenant Samson made the first British take-off from a warship. The *Africa* was at anchor off Sheerness and the aircraft landed alongside where it floated gently on the calm water.

The practical value of naval flying allowed the Admiralty to draw up a wartime requirement for aircraft – they should be able to see what enemy vessels were in port; take off from a floating base; and fly over the Fleet to locate submarines, detect minefields and direct gunfire.

On 2 January 1912, Lieutenant Hugh A. Williamson, a submariner who had qualified as a pilot (Certificate No. 160, 28 November 1911), submitted another revolutionary paper, 'The Aeroplane in use against Submarines', in which he proposed the use of aircraft for detecting submarines and destroying them by bombs which would explode underwater. The seeds of an idea which grew into the invention of the aerial depth-charge, had been planted. Meanwhile, Samson and his colleagues were experimenting with crude bomb sights and Lieutenant Raymond Fitzmaurice had been appointed to conduct experiments in wireless telegraphy. On 11 March 1912, Longmore flew a distance of 181 miles in 3 hours 15 minutes to win the Singer £500 Naval Prize, and on 7 May was appointed to HMS *Hermes* for Command of Cromarty Naval Air Station, which then existed only on paper. The first naval revolution in aviation technology was just beginning.

Samson had been working with Horace Short on the design of a seaplane, and the first had been completed in March for trials off Portland. This was the Short S41 biplane with single-step mahogany floats. It flew over 150 hours without accident and was demonstrated by Samson at the Fleet Review in Weymouth Bay during May. This aircraft was later taken over by the Navy with serial No. 10. Two modified S41s (Nos 20 and 21) were flown by Flight Sub-Lieutenant J. T. Babington in wireless experiments, and signals were received by Samson over a range of 4 miles while flying off Harwich.

On hearing that Samson might be thinking of experimenting with deck landings, an early aviation writer commented: "He is not only one of the most magnificent flyers in the country, but he is an exceedingly valuable officer and a man of very considerable mental ability and should not, therefore, be permitted to risk his life on what is, after all is said and done, simply a dangerous trick . . . of no practical value whatever."

The Royal Flying Corps was officially constituted on 13 April 1912 and resolved itself almost immediately into two separate entities, the RFC Military and Naval Wings.

On 9 May, Gregory's pioneering thrust resulted in the world's first take-off from a ship under way. He flew a modified S27 off a platform built over the forecastle of HMS *Hibernia* when she was steaming at 10½ knots with the wind dead ahead Force 1, the aeroplane rose after a run of only 45 ft. Another Short biplane that year flew from the forecastle of HMS *London*, when she was steaming at 12 knots into a Force 3 wind. This time the Short rose after a mere 25 ft. Lieutenants Gregory, L'Estrange Malone, Longmore and Major Gerrard, also took part in the flying display at the Fleet Review.

These three photographs show the general appearance of the platform built over the forecastle of the *Hibernia*, and the Short biplane rising from the ship. Commander Samson is seen right after landing at Lodmoor.

There were now 22 officers in the Naval Wing including 8 with aviator certificates. The officers included Captains Paine, and Sueter; Commanders Swann, Masterman, and Samson; Captain R. Gordon, RMLI; Temporary Major Gerrard, RMA; Lieutenants Gregory, Longmore, Usborne, L'Estrange Malone, Boothby, Seddon, Woodcock, Parke, S. D. Gray, and Fitzmaurice, with Engineer Lieutenants E. F. Briggs and C. J. Randall. Engine Room Artificer F. W. Scarff, the inventor of the first movable gun mounting – socket, pillar and Scarff ring – was also borne on the books.

On 19 June the Central Flying School opened at Upavon and Captain Godfrey Paine, CB, MVO, RN, was appointed as the first Commandant to date 25 July. Longmore and Gerrard were appointed as Instructors. On 7 June S. F. Cody was killed when his aircraft crashed coming in to land on Laffan's Plain, Farnborough, just 12 days before the first course started at CFS with 6 RN/RM officers reporting for training. Although the school was supposed to train all Service pilots, the Navy retained their own school at Eastchurch, and Commander Samson was appointed to command it in November.

On 29 August 1912, Captain Sueter proposed the gradual establishment of a chain of flying stations round our coasts which were within easy flight of each other, and strategically placed to protect bases and coastal shipping traffic. On 2 November they were all approved by Admiralty (with the exception of Weybridge), together with the additional stations of Weymouth, Scapa Flow and the Clyde.

Stations and notes (alphabetical order)

Aberdeen	Harwich (2 sheds established)
Cleethorpes	Newcastle
Cromarty	Pembroke
Cromer	Portsmouth (2 sheds established)
Dover	Plymouth
Filey	Rosyth (3 sheds being established)
	Sheppey (Eastchurch Flying School)

Winston Churchill had earlier given approval for stations at the Isle of Grain and Calshot. Sueter's proposals also included Naval Airship Stations at Chatham (Teapot Head), the Norfolk Broads area and Rosyth. These were also approved.

Already, however, a new figure had come on stage – one who was to dominate the aviation scene for years to come – Major Hugh Trenchard. He had completed his flying training at Brooklands under Mr Copland Perry and, although never a brilliant pilot, completed the course after only 90 minutes of actual flying time, in two weeks. On 13 August 1912 he was awarded Certificate No. 270. Trenchard then reported to CFS where Captain Paine selected Longmore and Gerrard as his instructors. Almost before he realized what was happening, Paine persuaded Trenchard that because the Army outnumbered the Navy trainees by some 3 to 1, the School needed an Army Adjutant to avoid conflicting Service interests causing trouble. Ironically, the post also carried the extra duties of School Examiner. The few machines then at Upavon were a mixed bag of Shorts, Avros, with Bleriot monoplanes and Farman 'Longhorns' for the trainees.

The stage was being set for the clash of wills, dominated by inter-Service rivalries, that was to follow the setting up of the RAF with its first Air Marshal, Trenchard, opposing Admiral Sir David Beatty and the Admiralty's attempt to regain control of its own air arm.

The unmistakable figure of Hugh Trenchard (3rd left back row) next to Captain Godfrey Paine, with Samson (2nd left front row) and Gerrard (extreme right).

Right from the start, Trenchard showed all his energy and enthusiasm in his new job. In September 1912 he had flown as an observer with Longmore and succeeded in locating Haig's advancing forces during the Army exercises. Within an hour the information was back in the hands of the opposing force Commander, General Grierson. Longmore and Trenchard then flew with orders to General Briggs, the Cavalry Commander, and the opposing force gained a valuable initiative. This incident emphasized the importance of aircraft for reconnaissance. At the school he also set examinations in map-reading, rudimentary engineering and air observation. He sat and passed the same exams himself. During these formative years Winston Churchill was First Lord and from the beginning expressed a strong belief in the future of naval aviation. He personally suggested the modification of seaplanes with folding wings so they could be stored more easily, and as seaplane experiments grew throughout 1912, the first coastal seaplane station was opened. The station on the Isle of Grain facing the great Naval Dockyard of Chatham across the River Medway, was also the first RNAS Experimental Station. It commissioned on 31 December 1912 under the command of Lieutenant J. W. Seddon and became the centre for the folding wing experiments. On several occasions Seddon flew Winston Churchill on the 16-mile (25 kms) trip from Gravesend to Grain so that he could keep abreast of the latest designs. Seddon recalled in one report that although flying just above the water to avoid gale force winds, the trip took nearly an hour.

The Navy lost two early chances in December 1912 and the summer of 1915, to lead the world with the 'island' type carrier. The earliest mention of a carrier as we know it seems to stem from the book by Clement Ader, *L'Aviation Militaire*, first published in 1909. Although it caused little comment at the time and certainly no nation took it up, Ader wrote that a ship able to carry aircraft, and fast enough to operate with the Fleet, was essential for naval operations. With great foresight he added that the deck should be clear of all obstructions with the aircraft stowed away beneath decks.

In December 1912, after consultations with Sueter, the famous shipbuilding firm of William Beardmore, Dalmuir, Scotland, submitted unique designs for a similar type of carrier. It was examined by the Admiralty who later recommended a joint meeting of company and technical Naval representatives, to examine and improve the design. For some obscure reason this meeting never took place. In the summer of 1915, Lieutenant Williamson, the submariner, submitted revolutionary designs for an 'island' carrier with a flush deck and all the superstructure on one side. He envisaged converting a big ocean liner, but the idea was again too daring for a hard-pressed Admiralty, and Sueter was persuaded to accept the Argus compromise.

The basic launch platform stems from the early trials carried out by Eugene Ely on 14 November 1910, when he flew a Curtiss 'pusher' aircraft with a 50-hp engine off a wooden platform built over the bows of the cruiser uss *Birmingham*. For the trials on 8 January 1911, the 13,600-ton armoured cruiser uss *Pennsylvania* was modified with a wooden platform 110 ft (30 m) long and 30 ft (9 m) wide, built over her stern. There were 22 transverse 'arrester' ropes spaced at about 3 ft (1 m) intervals with 50 lb (23 kgs) sandbags attached to each end. Ely landed safely on the platform after catching the last 12 ropes with ease, and an hour or so later, took off again and landed safely back on shore. The case for the carrier had been successfully demonstrated. Governments and military chiefs in general only envisaged aircraft being of value for reconnaissance, and the development of floatplanes for the Navy was given precedence, in order not to interfere with the fighting qualities of warships. Space was still a major factor, and the Short Brothers folding-wing principle was needed before the use of landplanes at sea could be considered seriously.

In December 1912 it was reported that 3SL was considering a depot ship for destroyers and submarines that would carry six floatplanes ready for use and four more as spares. HMS *Hermes* was eventually selected. Experiments to design a folding wing were proceeding.

On 11 December 1912, Lieutenant Parke – who had done so much in these pioneering days – became the first naval air fatality when he was killed piloting a Handley Page monoplane from Hendon to Derby.

The Naval Wing continued to expand rapidly in 1913 and on 19 January, Lieutenant C. L. Courtney (later ACM Sir Christopher) from the battleship HMS *Commonwealth*, was graded Flying Officer. On 14 February, Royal Sanction was given to the Navigation Act 1911, forbidding the overflying of defended ports.

The draft Naval Estimates contained the first mention of a Naval Aviation Service with seaplane stations at the Isle of Grain and Sheerness; Naval Flying School at Eastchurch; airship base at Kingsnorth Farm, Chatham, and a joint Central Flying School on Salisbury Plain. The proposed expenditure for 1913–1914 reached £350,000, including £50,000 for 35 additional aircraft, £20,000 for improving the Isle of Grain, and £10,000 for Cromarty.

The Admiralty ordered two Sopwith Tractor biplanes on 13 February and these were collected by Spenser Grey and L'Estrange Malone. In April the Admiralty announced construction of a Naval Air Station at Felixstowe, and this commissioned on 5 August 1913, under the Command of Squadron Commander C. E. Risk. Three seaplane sheds were constructed and other famous COs included Lieutenant C. E. Rathbone, RMLI, 1914–1915, and Commander J. C. Porte 1915–1918.

On 1 April Lt T. S. Cresswell was appointed to HMS *Actaeon*, additional as Flying Officer Yarmouth Naval Air Station, which commissioned on the 15th. On the 13th Lt Gregory was posted to *Actaeon*, additional as Squadron Commander to command Yarmouth Group of Naval Air Stations, and Lt C. L. Courtney joined as Flight Commander. On the 10th Lt Spenser Grey commissioned Calshot.

The first graduates from CFS on 16 April included several pilots destined for high honours: Lts D. A. Oliver, J. R. Kennedy, H. D. Vernon and R. P. Ross, RN; Lt F. Bowhill, RNR (later ACM Sir Frederick); Sub-Lts A. W. Bigsworth, RNR (later Air Commodore), R. G. Marix, H. A. Littleton, RNVR, and Lt C. E. Rathbone, RMLI.

On 7 May 1913, the *Hermes* commissioned in succession to the *Actaeon* as headquarters and parent ship of the Naval Wing (Captain G. W. Vivian), and the term Air Mechanic was used for the first time in manning. The *Hermes* had been specially fitted to carry seaplanes, with an upper deck clear of all obstructions and running flush from the stem to 100 ft (30 m) aft. Further aft was a spacious hatchway leading to a large hold for stowage, with a workshop built around the hatch on the upper deck. Two power-operated cranes were fitted, one on either side of the deck. Her speed of only 10 knots, however, limited her ability to operate with the Fleet. From the experimental trackway, an 80-hp Caudron amphibian made several flights in the Spring. It used a wheeled-trolley for take-off and this was jettisoned on leaving the deck. The *Hermes* carried and launched two seaplanes in this way and after landing on the sea, they were winched back inboard by the cranes.

The difficulty of getting seaplanes airborne in the open North Sea in anything but the rare and seldom experienced perfect conditions, was to prove a constant embarrassment during the war. It led to a long series of protracted flying trials and the opportunity for the Royal Navy to exploit air power effectively at sea was lost. Nevertheless, the *Hermes* experiments were promising and gave added impetus to the development of the Short Folder – one of the earliest aircraft in the world with folding wings to conserve space and facilitate stowage on board. The first Folders were Nos 81 and 82 which were very similar to the earlier S41s with two-bay wings.

Wireless experiments continued and in May, while escorting the Royal Yacht back from the German wedding in Short seaplane No. 20,

Sub-Lieutenant J. T. Babington sent the Navy's first airborne salute to the King. Signals were received at the Isle of Grain 50 miles (80 kms) away.

On 31 May, Lieutenant Courtney flew the Farman aeroplane No. 69 and became the first naval pilot to land at Yarmouth Naval Air Station.

On 10 July 1913 the Admiralty announced the historic fleet manoeuvres when aircraft were used with the Fleet for the first time.

Red Fleet had HMS *Hermes* with two S41s, Cdr Samson and Lt-Cdr Gregory on board, and Yarmouth Air Station with 4 machines – Short No. 20 with W/T and Borel No. 84 (seaplanes), and Maurice Farman aeroplanes Nos 67 and 84. Pilots included: Lts Courtney and Seddon, RN, Cresswell, RMLI, and Sub-Lt Hewlett.

Blue Fleet had the air stations at Leven (Firth of Forth) and Cromarty commanded by Lt Longmore, whose pilots included Captain Gordon and Lieutenant Rathbone, RMLI, and Lieutenant Oliver, RN.

Shortly after these successful manoeuvres the First Lord (Winston Churchill) announced in The House on 17 July 1913, the use of the word seaplane for an aircraft taking off from the sea. On 21 July, Samson flew Short Folder No. 81, the first British aircraft with folding wings, off the forward platform of the *Hermes*. In the same month, Lt R. H. Clark-Hall (later AM Sir) was put in charge of aircraft armament experiments.

The increasing efficiency of early W/T communications was dramatically emphasized on 1 August when Samson (pilot) and Lt Raymond Fitzmaurice (observer) were forced to land on the sea in Short No. 81. Before landing they were able to send a W/T message through to the *Hermes* from which the aircraft's position was determined and HMS *Mermaid* was detailed to search for the seaplane. The crew had already been picked up by the German ship *Clara Mennig*.

On 13 August the Air Department issued its first General Order, 'Instructions for the conduct of Naval Air Stations', in which mention was made of the *Hermes* as the parent ship of the Naval Air Service. This appears to be the very first occasion on which a Naval Air Service was referred to. The Commanding Officer of the *Hermes* (Captain G. W. Vivian) was also appointed to take charge of all Naval Air Stations, and on 2 September all ranks of the RNAS were transferred to the books of the *Hermes* except for those at CFS, who were borne on the books of HMS *President*.

The Order also reported on stations established or being established with those in the same Naval Group being placed under the command of the Principal Air Station of the Group (PASG).

Station	Group	PASG
Scapa Flow		
Cromarty		
one other	Cromarty	Cromarty
Rosyth		
two others	Rosyth	Rosyth
Newcastle	Newcastle	
Cleethorpes	Cleethorpes	
Yarmouth	Yarmouth	Newcastle
Harwich		
Isle of Grain		
Dover	Sheerness	Isle of Grain
Chatham Airship Station		
Calshot (instructional and experimental)		

The disposition of the Naval Wing RFC at 1 May 1913 and the officers employed were approximately as under.

Admiralty Air Department

Captain M. F. Sueter	Director
Commander O. Schwann	
Lieutenant C. L'Estrange Malone	Assistants
Engineer Lieutenant G. W. S. Aldwell	Engineering Inspector

Naval Flying School, Eastchurch

Commander C. R. Samson	In command
Lieutenant R. Bell Davies	First Lieutenant

Seaplane Stations (open or scheduled) Grain, Calshot, Harwich, Yarmouth

Lieutenant R. Gregory	Sqn Cdr Yarmouth Group
Lieutenant C. L. Courtney	Yarmouth Flt Cdr
Lieutenant T. S. Cresswell, RMLI	Yarmouth Flying Officer
Lieutenant Commander Spenser Grey	Calshot in command
Lieutenant J. W. Seddon	Isle of Grain in command

Naval Airship Section

Commander E. A. D. Masterman	In command Farnborough
Lieutenant F. L. M. Boothby	
Lieutenant N. F. Usborne	
Lieutenant F. A. P. Freeman Williams	
Lieutenant H. L. Woodcock	Attached for experience

Aircraft (approximate numbers)

7 monoplanes	–	Bleriot, 2 Deperdussin, 1 Etrich, 1 Nieuport, 2 Shorts
15 biplanes	–	1 Avro, 2 Bristol, 1 Breguet, 1 Caudron, 2 H.Farman, 1 M.Farman, 5 Shorts, 2 Sopwith
10 seaplanes	–	1 Astra, 1 Avro, 2 Borel, 1 Donnet-Leveque, 1 H.Farman, 1 M.Farman, 3 Shorts

Qualified Pilots

Squadron Commanders:	Capts E. L. Gerrard and R. Gordon, RMLI; Lts R. Gregory, C. L'Estrange Malone, A. N. Longmore; Cdr C. R. Samson; Lt P. A. Shepherd.
Flight Commanders:	Lt I. T. Courtney, RMLI; Lt Spenser Grey; Captain C. E. Risk, RMA; Lt J. W. Seddon.
Flying Officers:	Lts J. T. Babington, A. W. Bigsworth, F. W. Bowhill, C. L. Courtney, R. B. Davies, G. H. Edmonds; Sub-Lt F. E. J. Hewlett; Lts J. B. Kennedy, E. A. Oliver, C. E. Rathbone, RMLI, R. P. Ross, J. L. Travers, H. D. Vernon, G. V. Wildman-Lushington, RMA.
Not on Flying Duties wholetime but employed Admiralty, CFS or Eastchurch:	Lt J. C. Andrews; AB P. E. Bateman; Lt T. S. Cresswell, RMLI; Assistant Paymaster H. J. Lidderdale; ERA T. O'Connor; Captain G. M. Paine, RN; Eng. Lt C. J. Randall; Commander O. Schwann; Shipwright D. Shaw.
Private Licences:	Lts J. A. Bower, R. H. Clark-Hall, Williamson, H. A. Williamson, G. Blatherwick; Cdr A. M. T. Brown; Lt C. H. Edwards, F. A. Freeman Williams, G. G. W. Head; Sub-Lt C. W. W. Hooper; Cdr E. A. D. Masterman; Lt C. B. Prickett; Assistant Paymaster G. Trewin; Lt N. F. D. Usborne; Midshipman N. F. Wheeler; Lts F. L. M. Boothby, B. J. Brady, A. C. G. Brown, W. F. Dobie, R. Fitzmaurice, S. T. Freeman; Sub-Lt H. A. Littleton; Lts W. Pickton-Warlow, R. P. Ross.
Under Instruction:	Lt A. W. Agar; WO H. C. Bobbett; Lt F. G. Broadribb; Captain H. Fawcett, RMA; Lts A. B. Gaskell, C. E. Maude; Assistant Paymasters C. R. F. Noyes, E. B. Parker; Lt W. G. Sitwell.

In the first annual report of the Air Committee of 7 June 1913, it was reported that the Admiralty had found it necessary to establish an Air Department, and that the personnel trained or under training were:

Establishment	Trained	Under training
Eastchurch	24 officers	1
	41 men	80
Farnborough	5 officers	3
	30 men	30
CFS	20 officers	64 men

There were 34 naval aircraft of various types and 68 were on order of which 55 were seaplanes. Five large double sheds had been erected at Eastchurch and a hydroplane station on the Isle of Grain. Sheds had or were being built at Calshot, Harwich, Yarmouth and Rosyth. Further sheds were needed at Dover, Cleethorpes, Newcastle, Peterhead, Cromarty, and Scapa Flow.

Twenty hydroplanes had been fitted with W/T as were the Parseval and Astra-Torres airships. It had been decided to adopt wheel warping and foot steering for all naval machines.

Naval Air Expenditure was reported as: 1911 £50,000; 1912 £141,000 and 1913 estimated at £321,600.

Churchill continued to be heavily involved in the organization and administration of the Naval Wing, and in August 1913 he wrote to 2SL advocating the direct entry of civilians to the Navy Wing, at the age of 24. They ought to receive a pension or lump sum after 10 years or be offered permanent employment in the Navy. No officer should expect to fly aeroplanes for more than 5 years and if they wanted to continue in the Air Specialization, they must look to the Airship Section for the second part of their career.

On 12 November he was writing that the bases on which to concentrate work should now be Fort George (Lt Longmore) with personnel from the Firth of Forth; Harwich and Yarmouth (Lt Gregory), the Isle of Grain and Calshot. He suggested an annual summer exercise at Grain which should become the Principal Seaplane Station.

In December Churchill first mentioned the need for an Air Service Training Manual, and on the 5th of that month the Naval Air Service was placed under the Administrative control of 4SL, Captain C. F. Lambert (later Admiral Sir Cecil).

The Avro 504 made its debut at Hendon on 20 September 1913 and on 20 November at Farnborough when it flew at 80.9 mph over the measured mile and climbed to 1,000 ft in 1 min. 45 secs. It was widely used by front-line squadrons of the RNAS and RFC for bombing and reconnaissance, but in 1915 reverted to the training role. The Admiralty ordered one in 1913 but wanted wing spars of greater cross-section and this greatly modified version was known as the Avro 504B. The 504K first appeared early in 1918 with modified engine bearers so that a variety of rotary engines could be fitted, including the 110-hp Le Rhône, the 130-hp Clerget and the 100-hp Monosoupape. In the training role it became one of the most famous aircraft of the period. It was standard equipment until the 504N arrived with a Lynx engine. The last production order was placed on 17 January 1927.

Early on in the famous Avro 504 series, like the 504A above, wing
warping had given away to normal ailerons and a more streamlined
cowling. For the time, it was a good-looking aircraft with a splendid
performance which was only bettered by the Sopwith Tabloid, its main
rival. When war broke out, the RNAS only had one on its strength but
by December, 1 Squadron (Squadron Commander A. M. Longmore)
had more and by the time they relieved Samson's Eastchurch Squadron
in February 1915, they had six on their strength. The 504A was used in
the devastating early raids on the Zeppelin sheds. The 504B was used
almost exclusively as a trainer and, like other naval variants such as the
B, C, G, replaced the 'comma' tail of other 504s with the vertical tail
and long-span ailerons. The G was a gunnery trainer, armed with a
single fixed Vickers forward and a single Lewis on a Scarff ring aft.

The series had a wing span of 36 ft (11 m), length of 29 ft 5 in. (9 m)
and a height of 10 ft 5 in. (3.2 m). Maximum speed was 82 mph (71
knots) at sea level and they could climb to 3,500 ft (1,067 m) in 7
minutes. Loaded weight was 1,574 lb (715.5 kg), endurance 4 hours 30
minutes, and the armed versions carried four 20-lb (9 kg) bombs.

Avro 504B on a training flight, RNAS Chingford 1917.

The Sopwith Three-seater Tractor biplane above, appeared the same time as the Bat Boat in 1913 and seated two in the front cockpit with the pilot in the rear one. At the start of the war the RNAS had six of them; two went to Dunkirk with the Eastchurch Squadron, while the others carried out war patrols from Great Yarmouth. They had a span of 40 ft (12 m), length of 29 ft (9 m) and loaded weight of 1,550 lb (704.5 kg).

The first trainer variant was the 504B, which was followed in service by the 504E with a more powerful 100-hp Gnome Monosoupape engine and an auxiliary fuel tank in place of the front cockpit, to give an endurance of 8 hours for long-range reconnaissance. The B variant did pioneer work on deck arrester gear. In 1918, the J was superseded by the 504K – some of which were converted Js – and this was in use at former FAA training schools and remained as an FAA trainer until the early 1920s. All naval pilots did their preliminary training at Netheravon, and at Leuchars where SR pilots were trained. For anti-Zeppelin patrols, some Cs were fitted with a Lewis gun firing upwards through the centre section. Some of the final combat versions of the K were single-seat night fighters. Various marks served with 1, 3 and 4 Squadrons, No. 2 Wing, and at training schools. A converted C, now known as the H, was used for early catapult trials in 1917.

Wing-walking on a 504N was a new experience for No. 2 Flying Training School, Digby.

Experimental 504K used by RAE Farnborough (above) and a 504N aircraft of the 1920s developed from the series.

The Sopwith Tabloid was winner of the Schneider Trophy contest in 1914; some of their famous exploits during the war are recounted later on in this book. Powered by a 100-hp Gnome Monosoupape, it had a span of 25 ft 6 in. (8 m), a length of 20 ft 4 in. (6 m) and height of 8 ft 5 in. (2.5 m). Loaded weight: 1,120 lb (509 kg). It was armed with a centre-section Lewis and could carry 20 lb (9 kg) of bombs.

Several aircraft were fitted with dual control, so that one pilot could relieve the other for long-range reconnaissance. On 29 November 1913, Harry Hawker demonstrated the Sopwith Tabloid at Hendon where it caused a sensation. With a top speed of 92 mph (72 knots), and able to climb at 1,200 ft a minute, this single-seater was in a class of its own. Production for the RNAS and RFC began early in 1914.

In December Lieutenant Travers designed a bomb sight with a clockwork motor, which could be fixed to an aircraft to measure its speed relative to a target, and on 31 December, Commander F. R. Scarlett was promoted to Captain and appointed in general charge of all Naval Air Stations as the first Inspecting Captain of Aircraft (later AVM High Speed Flight which won the Schneider Trophy in 1927).

As if with 1939 in mind, Churchill stated that the Naval Wing must have a proper proportion of good land-fighting aeroplanes if it were to compete on equal terms in any future aerial war. He told 4SL that Army airships should be concentrated at Kingsnorth, and aeroplanes and seaplanes at Calshot, Grain, Eastchurch, Yarmouth and Harwich. Cromer should not be proceeded with beyond supplying land and a shed.

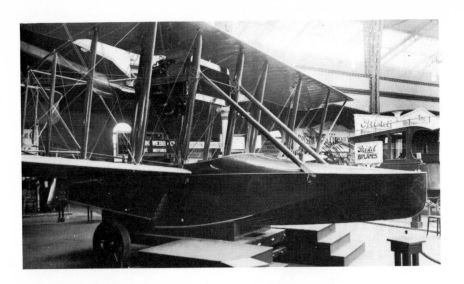

The Sopwith Bat Boat was the first flying boat built in the UK and took part in the Fleet Review of July 1914. During the war it was used for patrols from Scapa Flow and had a maximum speed of 65 mph (56 knots). Its span was 41 ft (12 m), its length 32 ft (10 m) and all-up weight 1,700 lb (773 kg).

The Sopwith Bat Boat, the first flying boat purchased by the Admiralty, was used for armament and night-flying experiments by Lieutenants Travers and A. Bigsworth. On 31 May 1914, armed with a Maxim gun and flown by Bigsworth, it was used in an attack on a flag target towed by HMS *Nubian*. Some 200 rounds were fired and 60 hits were scored. At Eastchurch a Sopwith Tractor was modified with a machine-gun mounted on a pillar between two tandem-cockpits, and firing upwards through a cut-out in the top wing trailing edge. Lieutenant R. Warner and W. O. J. Brownridge also modified a Sopwith Tabloid later in the same year, to carry a Lewis gun mounted on the top wing.

On 28 June, piloting Bat Boat No. 118 from Calshot, Bigsworth made what is thought to be the first night flight by a naval aircraft. Using a 50-candle-power 4-volt car headlight on the wing tip and another shaded one in the bows, the flight lasted 20 minutes and was entirely successful.

The fledgling years of the RNAS started in January 1914 with Gregory, Engineer Lieutenant E. W. Riley and Mr F. White (Chatham Dockyard) developing the successful G-W-R wheeled float attachment to replace trolleys. Short seaplane No. 20 was used for the experiments

A Wight Twin seaplane (serial No. 1451), with two 200-hp Canton Unne engines, which served at Felixstowe.

and the trials passenger was ERA E. Hackney.

The Naval Aircraft Allocation List showed 120 aircraft and seaplanes. On 15 January, Longmore took over command of Calshot from Spenser Grey. Lieutenant Bigsworth was Second-in-Command; Lieutenant Edmunds was responsible for Administration and Flying Duties. The officers included Lieutenant Clark-Hall as the gunnery specialist. Clark-Hall had conducted several successful experiments using a Vickers semi-automatic 1½-pounder gun, mounted in a Sopwith pusher Bat Boat. This gun was later transferred to a Short S81 seaplane (No. 126). Later in 1915 it was used for experiments with a 6-pounder. Both trials proved impracticable. Lieutenant Travers was also at Calshot carrying out night-flying experiments. The total complement was 10 officers and 42 ratings.

On 24 February, Sueter submitted his draft proposals for the re-organization of the Naval Air Service, which, he said, was about to take a share in the military development of the RN, although still in the initial experimental stages.

It was proposed that all officers should have one year of sea-going experience before being selected for the RNAS, and that they should not be away from the Fleet for more than four years. It was essential for ratings to have sea experience early in their career and before selection as petty officers. Pioneer officers of the Naval Wing were to be considered for promotion irrespective of their position on the seniority list. Royal Marine officers could retain their full dress and mess kits if desired and a moustache was optional, but they were not to retain their uniform in the flying service, which would spoil uniformity throughout the RNAS.

Earlier, on 4 June, Lt T. S. Creswell, RMLI, was killed overflying the Solent, when the wings of his seaplane folded up.

On 1 July 1914, the Admiralty issued an instruction on 'The Royal Naval Air Service – Organization'. The RNAS would consist of the Air Department Admiralty, Central Air Office, Flying School Eastchurch, and Naval Air Stations. Civilians were eligible for direct entry as Flight Sub-Lieutenants but would be on probation until qualified. Officers appointed to the RNAS, who obtained the pilot licence of the RAC at their own expense, would be refunded the sum of £75 or lesser sum charged for their tuition.

At the Spithead Review 18–22 July, flights of seaplanes took part from Isle of Grain (Squadron Commander Seddon); Dundee (Squadron Commander Gordon, RMLI); Great Yarmouth (Squadron Commander Courtney); Harwich (Felixstowe) (Squadron Commander C. E. Risk); and Calshot (Squadron Commander Longmore). Eighteen seaplanes were moored out in lines with the Fleet, and among the officers taking part were: Captain Scarlett; Squadron Commanders Gordon, Clark-Hall, Risk, Seddon; Flight Commanders J. Babington, Rathbone, Oliver, Hewlett, Fausset, Barnby, Bowhill, Cull, Cave-Brown-Cave, Williamson, Kershaw, Sitwell, Fowler, Nansen, Broadribb, Busk, Stone; and Lieutenant Lord Edward Grosvenor. Land machine pilots included Squadron Commanders Samson, Marix, Bell Davies, Courtney and Peirse. The aircraft taking part included Short Folders, S41s, Maurice Farmans, Sopwith Tractor and Tabloid, BE2s, Avro biplane, Bristol Scout, Sopwith Bat Boat, and a 50-hp Short. The occasion was also the first demonstration by naval pilots of formation flying.

On 28 July 1914, a Short three-bay Folder from Calshot, piloted by Longmore, made the first successful drop of an air torpedo. Much of the pioneer work in adapting the 14-inch 900-lb torpedo for release from the air, and designing the carrier which fitted between the floats, was the work of Flight-Lieutenant Hyde-Thomson. The next day Churchill minuted DAD that the primary duty of naval aircraft was to fight enemy aircraft and thus afford protection against air attack. Machines were not to be needlessly wasted on ordinary scouting duties. On the staff at Great Yarmouth was Mr H. C. Bobbett, (Boatswain (g) RN), the first WO naval aviator.

THE TEST OF WAR 1914–1918

On the outbreak of war on 4 August, Claude Grahame-White offered his services and the aerodrome at Hendon to the Government, and Grahame-White became a Squadron Commander, and Hendon an RNAS Station. Officers joining as pilots were trained at the Bristol School, Brooklands, or at Hendon, before going to CFS or Eastchurch to complete their flying training, which ended with a seaplane course at Calshot.

On 5 August, Longmore and Gerrard reported to Admiralty and were ordered by DAD to requisition aircraft and engines from civilian enterprises or flying schools. Their haul included 3 Morane monoplanes, a Farman, a Sopwith, a Bristol and 3 Bleriots from Brooklands and Hendon. The next day from Eastbourne and Shoreham, they collected 2 Farmans and 2 Avros.

On 8 August cross-Channel patrols were ordered, and on the 10th, Samson set up a base at Skegness. The next day, Flight Commander D. Oliver set up a base at Scapa Flow and the Admiralty requisitioned 3 SE and Chatham Railway Company cross-Channel steamers, the *Empress, Engadine* and *Riviera* – for conversion to seaplane carriers. On the 13th, Flight-Lieutenant E. T. R. Chambers commissioned the first temporary overseas base at Ostend, to provide air cover for BEF transports to France.

On 25 August, Longmore was ordered by Sueter to raise all the aircraft he could and fly them to Dunkirk. He arrived in an RE5, the first aircraft to be built in any quantity by the Royal Aircraft Factory, Farnborough. Powered by a 120-hp Austro-Daimler engine, it had a top speed of 78 mph, was inherently stable and was later used in bombing raids. Longmore took over command of the base depot at St Pol.

On the 27th, Samson was ordered to Ostend with the Eastchurch Squadron to fly aircraft in a reconnaissance role for the Royal Marines. With him went Bell Davies, Courtney, Lieutenants W. L. and F. R. Samson (brothers), Engineer Lieutenants E. F. Briggs, Sippe, Dalrymple-Clark, Beevor, Rainey, and Lord Edward Grosvenor. Transport drivers and ratings were ferried over in HMS *Empress*. Aircraft included 2 BE biplanes with 70-hp Renaults; 2 Sopwith Tractor 3-seaters with 80-hp Gnomes; 2 Bleriot monoplanes with a 50-hp and 80-hp Gnome engine; a Bristol TB8 biplane with an 80-hp Gnome, a Short (Admiralty No. 42) developed from the S41 which it resembled, and the BE2A (No. 50) in which Samson arrived.

With the worsening situation in Belgium and the danger of the airfields being overrun, Samson was ordered back to England, but subsequently received an Admiralty telegram to remain at Dunkirk to carry out reconnaissance and anti-Zeppelin patrols. He set up base at Dunkirk on 1 September.

Churchill, with his drive and initiative, had encouraged the RNAS to develop along offensive lines, and it was the RNAS who carried out the first bombing raids of the war on the Zeppelin sheds at Düsseldorf and Cologne. Squadron Commander Gerrard was in command of the operational arrangements and liaison at Antwerp from which the raid was to start. (Air 1/671 has details of all the early RNAS operations.)

Back home, on 3 September 1914, the Cabinet ordered the Navy to take over the anti-aircraft defence of the country, and this led to the formation of the RNVR Anti-Aircraft Corps which came into existence on 9 October.

On 5 September, HMS *Ark Royal* was launched as the first British seaplane carrier able to carry up to 10 seaplanes. This 7,500-ton merchant ship had been purchased by the Admiralty while being built at Blyth. She was 352 ft long with a beam of 51 ft, and had a 130-ft flush deck forward. The engines and bridge were aft, together with a 130 ft by 45 ft hangar for seaplane stowage.

The genesis of the aircraft carrier proper lay in these early seaplane carriers, of which 13 saw service between 1914 and 1918. Hurried conversions proved too slow to operate with the Fleet and were operationally inefficient requiring calm seas to get seaplanes airborne. The faster ones had their own teething troubles, and the overall result was a long series of protracted flying trials. Throughout the war, the Grand Fleet had no effective carrier to operate with it.

The *Ark Royal* commissioned on 9 December under the command of Commander R. Clark-Hall, and on 1 February 1915 sailed from Sheerness to Tenedos to take part in the ill-fated Dardanelles campaign. Her speed of just over 10 knots was insufficient to create enough speed over the deck, and she reverted to a simple seaplane carrier, operating Wight pusher seaplane No. 176 with five-bay folding wing; Short 136 – a development of the Short Folder with a 200-hp Salmson engine; Sopwith Schneider single-seater Scouts with 100-hp Gnome Monosoupapes, and two crated Tabloids.

Churchill's aggressive policy started to show results and on 22 September 1914, the first bombing raid over enemy territory was flown by Gerrard, Collett, Marix and Spenser Grey. Only Collett found the airship sheds at Düsseldorf and attacked from such a low height that the safety fans of the bombs did not have time to unwind. He hit the shed but the bomb did not explode. All the aircraft returned safely.

On 9 October came the first real success of the strategic bombing campaign when Squadron Commanders Marix and Spenser Grey attacked Düsseldorf and Cologne airship sheds, in Sopwith Tabloids. The Navy only had three of them in service. For Marix in No. 168 the success was complete. He dived on Düsseldorf and dropped both 20-lb bombs with great accuracy. The shed roof fell in and the new Zeppelin Z9, still to make an operational flight, was completely destroyed. His Tabloid came under heavy fire and he was forced to land 20 miles from Antwerp when his petrol ran out. He returned to Antwerp by bicycle and car.

Spenser Grey was not so lucky. He left Antwerp in No. 167 while the town was being bombarded and arrived over Cologne in thick mist. Unable to find the airship sheds, he attacked the railway station in the centre of the town and landed back just after 16.00. Two hours later, a general evacuation was ordered and the party arrived at Ostend in two cars, on 10 October.

On 14 October, Longmore was told to form 1 Squadron at Fort Grange, Gosport, and Gerrard 2 Squadron at Eastchurch. Longmore had Bigsworth as his No. 1 (First Lieutenant) and the first Flight was formed by 4 Bristol Tractor TB8s from Farnborough. Courtney, Babington, Osmond and Sippe were among the pilots who joined the squadron. Later aircraft included 8 Avro 504s.

One of the most brilliant raids of these early days was the audacious one planned by Lieutenant Noel Pemberton-Billing on the Zeppelin sheds at Friedrichshafen which stood on Lake Constance, near the Swiss frontier. It was the centre for the Zeppelin enterprises. Pemberton-Billing arrived at Belfort on 24 October to finalize plans and returned to England on the 28th, to collect a flight of 4 Avro 504s built at Manchester, and supervised by Squadron Commander P. Shepherd. The pilots were Squadron Commander E. F. Briggs (No. 874), Flight Commander J. T. Babington (No. 875), Flight-Lieutenant S. V. Sippe (No. 873), and Flight Sub-Lieutenant R. P. Cannon (No. 179 and the first 504 to enter service with the RNAS). The aircraft were modified to carry 4 × 20-lb bombs each, and on the night of 13 November 1914 they arrived by train at Belfort. They were hidden in a barn.

On 21 November starting at 09.30 and leaving at intervals, Briggs, Babington and Sippe took off. Cannon's machine broke its tail skid and could not take part. The raiders flew at 5,000 ft along the Rhine, came in low over Lake Constance and attacked from 1,200 ft, hitting the target with several bombs. They destroyed a gas plant. Briggs was shot down and captured, but the others returned safely.

The old converted seaplane carrier, HMS *Hermes*, was torpedoed by a U-boat off Calais on 31 October, 1914.

A few days earlier on 26 October, Churchill had minuted DAD suggesting the use of the longest barges that could be found, to launch aeroplanes or seaplanes by means of a wheeled trolley and an accelerating windlass. The Admiralty also ordered 7 ft × 5 ft Union Jacks to be painted on the lower wings of all aircraft. These proved of little value, and on 11 December the RNAS adopted roundels for wings only of a red outer circle with a white centre.

An Admiralty memorandum to the Cabinet, dated 9 December, stated that Treasury approval had been given to an expansion costing £963,000. It included £525,000 for 300 extra aeroplanes with spares (£1,750 each); £288,000 for 96 seaplanes with spares (£3,000 each); £80,000 for 8 special seaplanes with spares (£10,000 each); and £70,000 for 14 Atlantic seaplanes with spares (£5,000 each).

On Christmas day 1914, the *Empress, Riviera* and *Engadine* launched the first ship-borne bombing attack of the war, when they set out to raid Cuxhaven. These small craft only displaced 1,670 tons and were 330 ft long with a beam of 41 ft. They could reach 21 knots and were equipped with canvas hangars capable of taking 4 aircraft, erected on deck. They had derricks for handling the various Short aircraft carried – Type 74s, Nos 812, 814 and 815 on the *Empress* (Flight-Lt F. W. Bowhill); Short Folders Nos 119 and 120 and Short 135s, Nos 135 and 136. A total of 9 Short aircraft were carried but only 7 started on the raid which was launched in a calm sea, but in bitterly cold weather, from a rendezvous 12 miles north of Heligoland. Heavy fog prevented the attack from being pressed home, but damage was done in the Port area and caused some panic among the German Fleet. Three of the raiders returned safely and were hoisted in to their parent ships. Three crews were picked up by the famous British submarine Ell, and the remaining crew were interned in Holland after landing near a Dutch trawler.

If 1914 had been a year of great achievement, 1915 was to prove a year of further advances and some disappointments. On 1 January, Longmore was promoted to Wing Commander and on 5 February, an Admiralty Weekly Order proposed a further reorganization of the RNAS, as the existing organization did not yield the best results. DAD was to become responsible for the whole of the Naval Air Service, and to the Admiralty for its administration. The post of Inspecting Captain of Aircraft was to be abolished and the holder appointed to DAD for inspection duties.

By 17 February, the *Ark Royal* was at Tenedos and her aircraft, commanded by Samson, were engaged in spotting for shore batteries and reconnaissance. On 26 February, No. 1 Squadron moved from Dover to Dunkirk and on 24 March and 1 April, their 504s bombed Hoboken Shipyard, near Antwerp, and destroyed two U-boats. On 2 March 1915, Samson was able to write a paper (AIR 1/672) setting out the various methods of attacking enemy targets by bombs, a subject about which the RFC could offer no advice.

On 3 April an Admiralty conference was chaired by Churchill, who referred to the urgent need to develop a large fleet of aircraft able to deal "smashing blows" at the enemy and deliver 2 or 3 tons of bombs in one raid, while torpedo bombers attacked ships in harbour. The conference was attended by DAD, Commodore Sueter; Captain Scarlett; Wing Commanders R. M. Groves (ADAD) and Longmore; and Squadron Commanders Courtney, Spenser Grey and J. C. Porte. In his paper, Longmore stated that the Curtiss seaplanes supplied by America were far from perfect and that they should not be used on active service again until further experience had been gained.

The Short 184 made history as a torpedo bomber, with nearly 700 being built for the RNAS, and served in nearly every theatre of war. It stemmed from Sueter's interest in the torpedo as a weapon of war when he was DAD. The aircraft also operated from the *Engadine* at the Battle of Jutland. The original Sunbeam 225-hp engine was later increased to the 275-hp of the Sunbeam Maori – with twin exhaust stacks.

It had a wing span of 63 ft 6 in. (19 m), length of 40 ft 7½ in (12 m) and height of 13 ft 6 in (4 m). All-up weight was 5,363 lb (2,438 kg), endurance of 2¾ hours and ceiling 9,000 ft (2,744 m). Instead of the torpedo it could carry up to 520 lb of bombs. Climb rate was 8 min 35 sec to 2,000 ft (610 m). One free-mounted Lewis gun aft.

Without the impetus of war, it is doubtful if the seaplane carrier would have developed so quickly. Three other conversions were the *Ben-My-Chree*, *Vindex* and *Manxman*. Of these, perhaps the *Ben-My-Chree* is the best known. Just over 350 ft long with a beam of 46 ft, she was armed with two 4-inch guns, a 6-pdr AA gun and could do 24 knots. Commanded by Squadron Commander L'Estrange Malone, she had room for four 2-seater torpedo float planes – Short 184s powered by a 225-hp Sunbeam Mohawk engine with a 14-inch torpedo between the floats. It was from the *Ben-My-Chree* on 12 August 1915, that Flight Commander C. K. Edmonds sighted and torpedoed from the air a Turkish merchantman put out of action earlier by the British submarine E14. Not content with being the first man in the world to torpedo a ship from the air, he repeated the feat on the 17th when he torpedoed a Turkish supply ship off Ak Bashi Liman.

Another remarkable 'first' was achieved by Flight-Lieutenant G. B. Dacre, flying a Short 184 from the *Ben-My-Chree*, which landed on the water with an engine defect. After repairs, he was taxying on the water when he torpedoed a Turkish tug.

A major step forward in carrier history was the conversion of the 18,000-ton *Campania*, which commissioned on 10 April 1915. She was 600 ft long with a beam of 65 ft, a speed of 23 knots, and was armed with six 4.7-inch guns and a 3-inch AA gun. She was designed to carry 10 aircraft. The *Campania* was found unsuitable for operations and was modified in 1916 with the fore funnel split and the original flight-deck of 120 ft was lengthened to 200 ft and passed between the funnels.

The Commanding Officer, Wing Captain Oliver Swann (later AVM Sir Oliver), reported that on 6 August, Flight-Lieutenant W. L. Welsh (later Air Marshal Sir William) flew a Schneider Cup seaplane off the flight-deck with the ship steaming at 13 knots into a wind of 13 knots. The wheels were released close to *Campania*. Captain Swann added: "A proposal to keep the wheels of the seaplanes running between rails or in grooved recesses is now finding favour among pilots."

The famous Fairey Company named their second type of aircraft, the first designed to operate from a seaplane carrier – the Fairey Campania. The aircraft operated from the *Campania* in 1917 and took off by using a wheeled trolley which was left behind when the aircraft became airborne.

The Fairey Campania was powered by a Rolls-Royce Eagle Mk4 of 250 hp, but after the prototype changes were made including a 275-hp Eagle 5, larger fin and rudder. Later models had a Maori 2 and finally, when the shortage of Eagle engines was overcome, the 345-hp Eagle 8. Wing span was 61 ft 7½ in (19 m), length 43 ft (13 m), and height 15 ft 1 in (4.5 m). Loaded weight varied from about 3,600 lb (1,636 kg) to 5,650 lb (2,568 kg) according to the engine fitted. Endurance was 4½ hours, ceiling 6,000 ft (1,829 m) and it could climb to 2,000 ft (610 m) in seven minutes. Speed was 85 mph (74 knots) at sea level. It was armed with a Lewis gun on a Scarff mounting and fitted with bomb racks below the fuselage. By October 1918, some 42 Campanias were still in service and, as late as 1919, 5 operated from the *Nairana* against the Bolsheviks.

The Royal Navy's expertise in the use of air power at sea was the envy of many foreign navies, particularly the USN who kept a very close watch on our progress during the war. For this reason, the Campania is important as the first aircraft specifically designed to operate from a 'carrier'. It takes its name from the fact that it was originally designed to operate from the *Campania*, a liner purchased and converted by the Admiralty to carry up to 10 seaplanes, with a 120-ft long flight-deck above the forecastle. This was later increased to 200 ft.

By the end of October 1918, the aircraft was serving in the *Campania*, *Nairana* and *Pegasus*, and at RNAS stations, Bembridge, Calshot, Dundee, Newhaven, Scapa Flow, Portland and Rosyth.

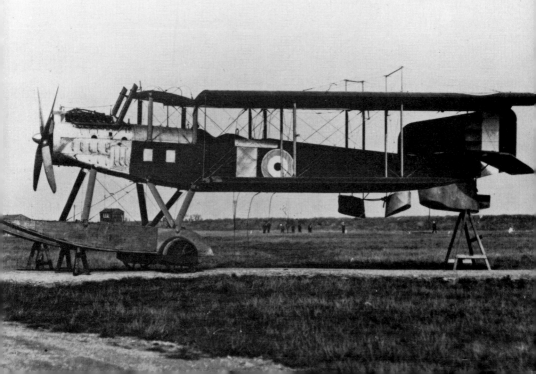

Turning from carriers for a moment, another remarkable first had occurred on 7 June when Flight Sub-Lieutenant R. A. J. Warneford was flying a single-seater Morane Parasol from Wing Commander Longmore's 1 Squadron at Dunkirk. The machine was armed with six 20-lb bombs and Warneford won the first VC for the RNAS when he 'bombed' and destroyed the Zeppelin LZ37, which was flying at a height of 10,000 ft over Ostend. The force of the explosion threw the monoplane on its back and Warneford landed behind the enemy lines with a fractured fuel pipe. He repaired it, took off and landed safely back at base. (Warneford was killed in a flying accident a short while afterwards.)

The remainder of the aircraft from 1 Squadron (almost immediately afterwards renumbered as No. 1 Wing, bombed and destroyed the Zeppelin LZ38 in the sheds at Evere. The pilots were Flight-Lieutenant J. P. Wilson and Flight Sub-Lieutenant J. S. Mills.

The Morane-Saulnier Type L above was the actual aircraft flown by Warneford, and the RNAS was the first British service to fly the type No. 2 Wing had six on their strength during the Dardanelles operation. Powered by an 80-hp Le Rhône, maximum speed was 76 mph (66 knots), and initial climb 345 ft a minute (105 m). Its wing span was 34 ft (10 m), length 20 ft 9 in (6 m), and height 11 ft 5 in (3.5 m). Improvised bomb racks, no armament.

On 1 August 1915, the reorganization of the RNAS took place and it became an integral part of the Royal Navy. The various air stations came under the general orders of the C-in-C or SNO in whose district they were situated. The 50 or so naval air stations were split into four groups for disciplinary and operational purposes.

The post of DAD was abolished and that of Director of Air Services substituted, with Rear-Admiral C. L. Vaughan-Lee as the first Director. Sueter was made Commodore 1st Class and appointed Superintendent of Aircraft Construction with two Assistants, Wing Commanders R. M. Groves and E. A. Masterman. There is little doubt that the appointment of a Flag Officer with no previous aviation experience over his head, must have been a bitter disappointment to Sueter and may have contributed to his decision later to support a Unified Air Force – while still serving in the Air Department.

On 25 August, Colonel F. H. Sykes (later Major-General Sir Frederick) took over Command of the RNAS as Wing Captain Commanding RNAS, Eastern Mediterranean Theatre – an appointment made over the head of the senior Naval Aviator, Wing Commander Samson, who was commanding No. 3 Wing. At about the same time, Wing Commander Gerrard arrived to take command of No. 2 Wing, and the aeroplane squadron moved from Tenedos to Imbros. This original No. 3 Wing was disbanded towards the end of December 1915 and reformed later in France.

On 3 November, Flight-Lieutenant B. F. Fowler flew a Bristol Scout (No. 1255) from the deck of HMS *Vindex** while she steamed into a head wind at 12 knots. The apparent wind speed over the deck was 27 knots, and the aircraft took off after an 'apparent run' of 46 ft (making allowances for the ship's movement and wind speed), and left the deck 18 ft from the stem.

On 22 November 1915, Squadron Commander R. Bell Davies (later Vice-Admiral Sir Richard, VC) won the second VC for the RNAS. Flying from No. 3 Wing he landed his single-seater Nieuport fighter behind the Turkish lines to rescue Flight Sub-Lieutenant G. F. Smylie (later Air Commodore) who had been shot down. As Turkish troops advanced towards them, Smylie destroyed his aircraft and anchored himself to the struts of Davies's Nieuport which took off with its double-load and landed back at base.

On 10 December, Godfrey Paine, CB, MVO, (later RA Sir Godfrey and AVM) was promoted Commodore 1st Class, to command the

*The *Vindex* was a converted Isle of Man steamer, *Viking*, of 2,900 tons and a speed of 22 knots, which had commissioned in September. The 64 ft long flight-deck and hangar forward was for the two fighters she carried and the after-hangar was for four large and a small seaplane.

RNAS Central Depot and Training Establishment, RNAS Cranwell. The staff were borne on the books of HMS *Daedalus*.

In reply to Wing Captain Sykes, who pleaded for urgently needed reinforcements, the Admiralty said on 14 December that 12 pilots, 6 Bristol Scouts, 2 Sopwith Scout seaplanes, and a Short seaplane had been sent. To follow were 15 Henry Farmans, 25 Nieuport 2-seaters, and 10 single-seaters, and in addition, one or two Bristol Scouts, Sopwith or Short seaplanes should arrive regularly, the first batch arriving in the *Empress* before the end of January 1916.

Samson's standing orders for No. 3 Wing, dated 4 December 1915, said pilots were to be armed with a revolver or pistol and carry binoculars and a safety device – either waistcoat, patent lifebelt or petrol can. Observers were always to carry a rifle. Almost as if with present day Recognition Training in mind, he added: "Don't open fire until you are certain it is a German. You must not open fire until you have seen the markings."

On 18 December at Hendon, the Handley Page 0/100 flew for the first time. Designed as a result of Murray Sueter's request for a "bloody paralyser" of an aircraft and to deal Churchill's "smashing blows" at the enemy, a total of 46 were built and the first production aircraft were delivered to No. 5 Wing, Dunkirk, November 1916. Powered by 2 Rolls-Royce Eagles or 320-hp Sunbeam Cossacks, it had a wing span of 100 ft, was 62 ft 10¼ in long and 22 ft high. It could carry up to 16 × 112-lb bombs and was armed with up to 5 free-mounted Lewis machine-guns. With a crew of 4, its top speed fully loaded was 85 mph.

Although the Bristol Scout pioneered the operation of landplanes from a carrier, the fertile minds of the RNAS were already working on many other brilliant ideas which were to lead to bitter controversy in 1916. A lot of night-flying experiments took place, and among ideas suggested was the painting of struts or other parts of an aircraft to avoid mid-air collisions; the use of luminous string instead of ordinary string as a side-slip indicator; and flares spaced at 400-yard intervals in an L configuration, as a landing aid. The flares led to diffused lights during final approaches and caused many crashes, so the experiments were temporarily terminated. To try and judge distance from the ground, even a weight at the end of a 50-yard long cord was tried. When the weight touched the ground, the pull on the cord triggered a switch in the cockpit, and switched on a warning light.

The agitation for co-operation between the two Arms grew in intensity. Many politicians viewed with alarm the situation in which they competed in the same markets for the same products and arising out of this conflict, opinion was forming for urgent reform concentrating first on the amalgamation of all existing production.

An Air Committee under Lord Derby was appointed on 15 February 1916, but was entirely advisory in character and failed (on 12 April) because it had no executive powers. On 17 May, an Air Board was appointed, again entirely advisory in character, headed by Lord Curzon. In August, without consulting this Air Board, the Admiralty obtained Treasury approval to spend over two million pounds on RNAS expansion. Curzon was outraged but his formal protest to A. J. Balfour, First Lord, only brought a reply from the Admiralty that they did not adjust their policy to suit the Air Board.

The Air Board then proposed that RNAS administration should be freed from Admiralty control, with supply, design, inspection and finance invested in the Air Board. Balfour's terse reply merely said: "I do not propose to discuss the constitution of the Admiralty. It was created some generations before the Air Board."

Ironically, the agitation was to be further inflamed by the Admiralty decision to create a long-range strategic bombing Wing operating from the French sector of the Allied lines. The Sea Lords agreed that with the RFC hard-pressed to provide adequate cover on the Western Front, the RNAS with its machines and trained personnel were best equipped to carry out long distance raids against targets such as blast furnaces and factories.

Early in 1916, the reorganization of RNAS Dunkirk had begun with the original No. 1 Wing expanding to Nos 1, 4 and 5 Wings. Wing Captain C. L. Lambe (later AVM Sir Charles) assumed command of the RNAS at Dover and Dunkirk and it was agreed to increase the Command to eight squadrons of 18 machines each, with a central repair depot at Dunkirk, and a local defence and training squadron at Dover. No. 1 Wing was at St Pol, No. 4 at Petite Snythe and No. 5 at Couderkerque. Under the reorganization, a Flight was 6 machines, a Squadron two or more flights and a Wing, two or more squadrons.

Caudron G IVs formed part of No. 4 Wing under Squadron Commander Courtney which arrived from Eastchurch on 11 April, to support No. 5 Wing under Squadron Commander Spenser Grey. The Wings combined on 2 August 1916, when 10 Caudrons and a Farman, with Sopwith 1½-Strutters as escort, took part in a massed daylight bombing attack on the German airfield at St Denis Westrem, near Ghent. The bombers attacked in line astern directed by Very lights fired by the escort – the pioneering example of the Pathfinder technique.

The Strutters were introduced into service on the Western Front by the RNAS and were the first with synchronized machine-guns firing forward through the propeller arc, and the first where both pilot and observer could use their guns most effectively and independent of each other. A single-seat version was developed for the RNAS with provision for 12 bombs to be stored internally. Powered by a 110-hp Clerget, they had a maximum speed of 106 mph, an endurance of 4½ hours, a ceiling of 13,000 ft and could carry two 65-lb bombs for A/S duties. The single-seater with a 130-hp Clerget could carry up to four 65-lb bombs.

No. 4 Wing for offensive patrols survived variously as 2 Squadron, B Squadron, and finally in November became 7 Squadron. It operated Short and Caudron bombers, and Sopwith Strutters, until moving to Couderkerque on 1 April 1917, when it was re-equipped with Handley Page 0/100s.

This single-seat version of the Strutter N5504 served with No. 5 Wing. The RNAS and the French were the only services to operate the type. During 1918, two-seat reconnaissance variants operated from capital ships of the Home Fleet. When war ended about 40 were with the Fleet and the *Furious*, Flagship Flying Squadron, carried 14.

Counters to the Zeppelin menace were being tried out and on 21 February 1916, Wing Commander N. F. Usborne and Squadron Commander de Courcy Ireland were killed trying out the idea of an 'airship aeroplane'. At about 4,000 ft, the BE2C slung beneath the airship envelope fell sharply away and turned on its back. Ireland fell into the River Medway where his body was later recovered by a lighter, and the aircraft crashed into the yard of Strood station killing Usborne.

On a happier note, a Bristol Scout from the *Vindex* (No. 3028), took part in a remarkable experiment with a Porte Baby flying boat which carried the Scout on its upper wing. The pilot, Flight-Lieutenant M. J. Day, operated a quick-release separation and successfully flew off the Scout. The flying boat was piloted by Porte. The experiment was not repeated.

Flight Commander Williamson, who had been injured in a crash while flying off the *Ark Royal* and was serving on the supply side of the Admiralty Air Department, designed an early type of arrester gear which was tried out at Grain Island. A large number of flexible steel wires were stretched in an inclined plane, fore and aft of a grid 200 ft long by 60 ft wide, representing a carrier's deck. Experiments proved that with only a slight head wind an aircraft with modified landing gear could be stopped 60 ft from the point of impact.

On 30 May, Sir David Beatty's battle-cruiser squadron had only one seaplane carrier available to operate with it, the *Engadine*. On 31 May 1916, the *Engadine* sent up a Westland-built Short 184 (No. 8359) piloted by Flight-Lieutenant F. J. Rutland with Assistant Paymaster G. S. Trewin as observer. They sighted the German Fleet and sent a wireless report to the *Engadine,* who was unfortunately unable to pass it to the Flagship. During the flight, the aircraft developed engine trouble and Rutland became the first man in the world to force land on the sea during a major naval battle. The *Engadine* came alongside and hoisted his seaplane inboard.

After Jutland, the Admiralty urgently considered the question of more carriers, better than the old *Manxman* – another hurried conversion – which had commissioned on 4 April 1916. Rutland was a passionate advocate of the greater use of wheeled undercarriages and the proper use of flight-decks.

An Admiralty minute by Sueter of 23 February on a proposed

Note: These experiments were terminated, as for effective operational use the arrester gear required specially built, high speed ships, and none was available.

Williamson (later Group Captain), whose earlier design of an aircraft carrier with all the structure on one side has already been mentioned, was later awarded £200 for his design of trollies for flying seaplanes off decks, and £500 for his brilliant 'island carrier' design. His model was very similar to that of HMS *Eagle*, completed 1923.

seaplane-carrying cruiser, stated that the requirements for flying off a ship's deck were understood, but of the *Engadine, Campania, Riviera, Empress, Ark Royal, Ben-My-Chree* and *Vindex,* only four – *Vindex, Ark Royal, Ben-My-Chree* and *Campania* – were suitable, the others being too small. Of the four, only *Campania* was suitable for conversion which would enable her to carry out a series of flights without stopping. The *Campania* was converted as already mentioned with a lengthened flight-deck.

Later, in September 1916, Lieutenant Commander G. R. A. Holmes and Wing Commander G. W. Aldwell reported on experiments with arrester gear for deck landings. They went back to the early design of the American trials, with 3 ropes, 20 ft apart, 6 inches off the ground, with a 30-lb sandbag on the end of each rope. The trials were carried out by flight-Lieutenant M. E. A. Wright, in an 80-hp Avro biplane, at Port Victoria Aeroplane Repair Yard which was opposite the Isle of Grain. The machine had a rigid hook designed to transmit the pull to the main part of the structure, and the trials were successful. It was said they promised a solution to operations from the Italian liner *Conte Rosso,* whose hull was purchased by the Admiralty in 1916. She was to emerge as HMS *Argus* in 1918, too late to take any part in the war.

The inter-Service squabbles erupted yet again when the Admiralty, on 27 July 1916, instructed Wing Captain W. L. Elder to begin strategic bombing when sufficient men and planes had been built up. He was to work directly under the orders of the French Military HQ, conform to their plans, and report directly to Admiralty on operations. Luxeuil was 200 miles from the nearest BEF position. Operations were delayed by an urgent request from the RFC for aircraft and the Wing handing over 62 Strutters to them. By October the Admiralty told the War Office that they had 47 aeroplanes and 45 pilots at Luxeuil.

Sir Douglas Haig, C-in-C BEF, complained bitterly that the Wing had been established and liaison arranged with French Military HQ without his knowledge or consent. In his opinion, the bombing of railways, enemy headquarters or barracks, and to destroy the enemy in the field, was of paramount importance. Strategic bombing was of minor importance. The Admiralty bowed to pressure and by 15 April 1917, the Wing had withdrawn to Dunkirk with four squadrons operating under RFC control, and a further 20 aircraft given to the French.

The various inter-Service rivalries such as this, resulted in the Admiralty decision to appoint a Fifth Sea Lord to represent them on the Air Board and to superintend the Air Department. His appointment was to be as Director of Air Services. On 3 January 1917, an Admiralty minute expressed the Board's appreciation to Rear-Admiral Vaughan-Lee on the termination of his appointment as DAS. The first Fifth Sea Lord was Rear-Admiral Godfrey Paine who was in post by 27 January and became a member of the second Air Board when it was established on 6 February 1917.

The Sopwith Scout – or Pup, as it became known – was like the Strutter, introduced into service on the Western Front by the RNAS. It began service trials with A Squadron (formed from Flights of No. 1 Wing) at Furnes, France. The aircraft first entered service in quantity with No. 1 Wing and on 25 October 1916, the famous Naval Eight (8 Squadron RNAS) was formed from a Flight each of Nos 1, 4 and 5 Wings. A Flight was six 80-hp Le Rhône Nieuport 17Bs; B Flight was six 80-hp Le Rhône Pups, and C Flight was six 110-hp Clerget Strutters.

The Squadron was formed following urgent representations by the Army Council for reinforcements on the Western Front. It operated with the Army until relieved by 3 Squadron on 7 February 1917.

During their three months with the RFC, operating from Vert Galand, Naval Eight destroyed 14 enemy aircraft and forced 13 down out of control. The Strutters had been replaced by Pups on 16 November 1916.

Squadron Commander G. R. Bromet (later AVM Sir) was the Commander of Naval Eight which handed its Pups to 3 Squadron on 1 February. By the middle of June, 3 Squadron had destroyed 80 German aircraft, and on return to the RNAS, was relieved by 9 Squadron who served with the RFC until 28 September 1917.

Sopwith Pup fitted with three Admiralty flotation bags doing ditching trials, Isle of Grain.

The Sopwith Pup pioneered true carrier operations. It was only 1,225 lb (557 kg) loaded, with a wing span of 26.5 ft (8 m), a length of 19 ft 3¾ in (6 m), and a height of 9 ft 5 in (2.9 m) with a top speed of 112 mph (97 knots) and a service ceiling of 17,500 ft (5,335 m). It was armed with a synchronized Vickers gun for land operations, but those operating at sea had a single Lewis gun firing upwards through a centre-section cut-out and a few had 8 Le Prieur rockets mounted on interplane struts.

On 28 June 1917, Squadron Commander Rutland flew a Pup off a 20-ft-long platform, fixed over the forward gun turret of HMS *Yarmouth*, while the ship was steaming into wind in the Firth of Forth. This was the first take-off from a turret platform built in a warship.

In July, the *Furious* (Captain Wilmot S. Nicholson), one of three fast battle-cruisers with 18-inch guns, rejoined the Fleet after conversion to a carrier. The forward gun turret had been removed and a hangar, surmounted by a flight-deck 228 ft (69.5 m) long and 50 ft (15 m) wide, was built over her forecastle. The 22,000-ton *Furious* had a top speed of 31 knots. On 2 August 1917, the Senior Flying Officer, Squadron Commander E. H. Dunning, flew a Pup off the flying deck and then made the first-ever landing on a ship under way. There was a strong but steady wind of 21 knots, with the ship steaming at 26 knots, giving an apparent wind of 47 knots. This was about the landing speed of the aircraft and there was no arrester gear other than the hands and arms of brother officers. Toggles had been fixed to the wing tips and tail of the Pup for deck-handling purposes. Dunning made his approach along the port side, side-slipped in and centred over the deck and landed in the right position. The aircraft was secured without too much difficulty. This magnificent achievement was to trigger off carrier developments and revolutionize naval warfare. Only five days later, while taking off for further trials, the engine of Dunning's Pup is believed to have stalled and he was blown over the side and drowned. There was no rescue destroyer or guard boat in those days. His historic flight is commemorated in the Dunning Trophy.

On 21 August, Flight Sub-Lieutenant B. A. Smart flew a Pup off the flying platform in the *Yarmouth* and shot the Zeppelin L23 down in flames off the Danish coast. This success led to the Admiralty having one light cruiser in each squadron fitted with a flying-off platform.

Another first was on 1 October 1917, when a Pup piloted by Rutland took off from a turntable platform built over a gun turret on HMS *Repulse*. This enabled the turret to be turned to launch the aircraft into the wind, irrespective of the ship's heading. The original platforms had been fixed.

The Sopwith Pup shown here is fitted with early-type arrester gear and skids, used in the deck-landing trials in the *Furious* below. The rigid skid undercarriage with 'dog lead' clips was designed to engage fore and aft arrester wires, an idea which persisted in the navy until abandoned in the 1930s.

The *Furious* suffered from a number of defects which caused experienced pilots difficulty when landing on. Nevertheless, on her next refit she was fitted with an early type of arrester gear and proved a valuable training platform for the design of future carriers.

By the end of February 1917, Naval Eight was re-equipped with 16 Sopwith Triplanes and on 28 March rejoined the RFC. The brief seven-month active service life of the Triplane, until it was superseded by the Sopwith Camel, was a remarkable success story. Famous 'aces' like Flight Sub-Lieutenant R. A. Little, Squadron Commander C. D. Booker (Naval Eight), and Flight Sub-Lieutenant Raymond Collishaw, made their names flying these aeroplanes.

Collishaw's B Flight of Naval Ten was the terror of the enemy between May and July when they destroyed 87 enemy aircraft. The all-black Triplanes bore names like Black Death, Black Maria, Black Prince and Black Sheep. Collishaw shot down 16 aircraft in 27 days, and on 27 June shot down the notorious German 'ace' Allmenroder.

The Sopwith Triplane, which was only operated by the RNAS, had a fast rate of roll and climb and was a major success in air combat. It only remained on operational service for eight months. Later versions had a smaller tail plane and 130-hp engine, to give better dive attack characteristics. Powered by a 110- or 130-hp Clerget, the Triplane had a wing span of 26.5 ft (8 m), length of 18 ft 10 in (5.8 m), a height of 10.5 ft (3 m), and a service ceiling of 20,500 ft (6,250 m). Initial climb: 25 minutes to 16,000 ft (4,878 m); loaded weight: 1,541 lb (700 kg); and maximum speed: 117 mph (101 knots). Normal armament: one fixed synchronized Vickers, but a few variants had two.

The Sopwith F1 Camel, the first British fighter with twin Vickers synchronized machine-guns, was the finest fighter of the war. First flown at Brooklands on 26 February 1917, it was used by both Services and the Camels in RNAS service accounted for 386 enemy aircraft destroyed. A prototype was evaluated at Dunkirk on 1 March and was also on trials with 9 and 11 Squadrons, until wrecked at Dunkirk on 20 August. It was to become a legend in its own lifetime, but one tends to forget because of its fighting achievements that it and the 2F1 – developed especially for the RNAS – took part in many pioneering naval experiments. They flew off towed lighters, were catapulted off gun turrets, flew from aircraft carriers and were also used in Italy and the Aegean. The power plant of the 130-hp Clerget was later updated to a 150-hp Bentley BR1. The F1 could carry four 25-lb (11.5 kg) bombs in racks below the wings, and the 2F1, two 50-lb (23 kg) bombs. The original task for the specialist ship Camel was Zeppelin interception over the North Sea, and it had a fuselage made in two parts for easier stowage on board ships.

The F1 had a wing span of 28 ft (8.5 m), a length of 18 ft 9 in (5.7 m), and a height of 8.5 ft (2.6 m). Service ceiling was 19,000 ft (5,793 m), maximum speed 115 mph (100 knots) at 6,500 ft (1,982 m), and climb 20 min 40 sec to 15,000 ft (4,573 m). Endurance was 2½ hours.

The 2F1 had a smaller wing span of 26 ft 11 in (8.2 m), a length of 18 ft 8 in (5.7 m), a height of 9 ft 1 in (2.75 m) and a maximum speed of 124 mph (108 knots) at 6,500 ft (1,982 m). Service ceiling was 17,500 ft (5,335 m), climb 25 min to 15,000 ft (4,573 m) and endurance 2½ hours. It was armed with one fixed Vickers forward and one Lewis gun mounted above the top wing centre section. All-up weight was 1,530 lb (696 kg).

The inventive genius of Squadron Commander Porte, who had taken over Command of Felixstowe in 1915, in his experiments and innovations with the H4 and H12 Curtiss flying boats, led to the widely-acclaimed Felixstowe-designed F2A. The Porte-designed hull incorporated the wing and tail assembly of the H12 and with its 6-hour endurance, 4–7 free-mounted Lewis machine-guns, and two 230-lb bombs, it was Porte's ideal weapon of war.

Although the H12 had a weak hull-planing section and take-off in anything but a fair sea was a risky affair, it was highly manoeuvrable and successful. On 13 April 1917, Felixstowe began its first H12 patrols and was followed by Great Yarmouth on 1 May, to start the famous 'Spider Web' patrols which allowed some 4,000 square miles of sea to be searched systematically for submarines.

Although earlier aircraft were powered by two 275-hp Rolls-Royce Eagles, later ones had the 345-hp Eagle 7 or 375-hp Eagle 8. This gave a maximum speed of 85 mph (74 knots) at 2,000 ft (610 m) and an endurance of 6 hours. Wing span was 92 ft 8½ in (28 m), length 46.5 ft (14 m), height 16 ft 6 in (5 m) and loaded weight 10,650 lb (4840 kg). Service ceiling was 10,800 ft (3,293 m).

On 14 May, an H12 from Great Yarmouth, with Flight Sub-Lieutenant R. Leckie (pilot) and Flight-Lieutenant C. J. Galpin (observer), shot down Zeppelin L22 some 20 miles off Texel Island and claimed the first ever destroyed by a flying boat.

On 14 June, this H12 from Felixstowe (below), with Flight Sub-

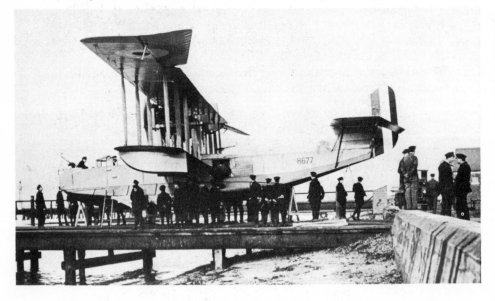

Lieutenant D. B. Hobbs (pilot) and Flight Sub-Lieutenant R. L. Dickey (observer), shot down the L43 off Vlieland.

On 20 May, Flight Sub-Lieutenants C. R. Morrish (pilot) and H. G. Boswell (observer), also flying an H12, bombed and destroyed the UC36, the first enemy submarine sunk from the air.

The flying boat saga would be incomplete without two actions in which the F2As took part. On 10 May 1918, N4291 from Killingholme with Captains T. C. Pattinson and A. H. Munday, attacked the L62 at 9,000 ft over the Heligoland minefields and shot it down in flames.

On 4 June 1918, in one of the greatest 'dog fights' of the war, a formation of four F2As and an H12 from Great Yarmouth and Felixstowe, attacked and shot down 6 out of 14 enemy aircraft. The only casualty was one F2A, forced down with engine failure before the engagement, and the H12 forced down (crew interned by the Dutch).

An F2A flying boat is seen on the slipway at Kalafrana, Malta, and below, a Sopwith Camel shelters beneath the lower wing of a flying boat.

This Strutter N5601 flies off on the straight and narrow path provided by a railed platform on HMS *Vindex*.

One suggestion of major interest was the remark by Wing Captain Swann (*Campania*) on 9 August 1917. The junior pilots sent to the ship, he said, seldom had sufficient flying experience; had never taken up a passenger before arrival; had very little knowledge of the compass for navigation, and little knowledge of starting, stopping or throttling down an engine. "The result is that considerable time is wasted in giving elementary practice work."

He submitted that pilots and observers intended for Fleet carriers should be instructed by using a two-seat tractor fuselage mounted on a revolving platform, permitting horizontal circular motion, and fitted with an engine producing sufficient slipstream to enable the fuselage to respond to the rudder. The fuselage was to be equipped with W/T and all other fittings so that it resembled a modern reconnaissance machine. It would be, in fact, an adaptation of the 'Teacher' used in the early days of flying. The first simulator had been suggested.

The first trials in the *Furious* had revealed that with the bridge superstructure and funnel left-amidships, pilots overflying to simulate landing on, often experienced turbulence caused by funnel gases and air flow eddies. Although the trials were abandoned, the idea of deck landings had gained favour and the *Furious* was taken in hand for conversion. A crude form of arrester gear, first tried out at the Isle of Grain, was installed during the refit at Newcastle. It consisted of longitudinal wires held about 9 inches above the deck. Twin horns fitted to the undercarriage were to engage the wires which would hold the aircraft on a straight line after landing. To stop forward motion there were transverse wires with sandbags at each end.

The after-turret, main mast and superstructure were removed and replaced with a 300-ft landing-on deck built over a hangar, and 25 ft above the quarter-deck. Fitted out like this the *Furious* rejoined the Fleet in March 1918, wearing the Flag of Rear-Admiral I. G. Phillimore (later Admiral Sir Charles), the first Admiral Commanding Aircraft.

On 18 July 1918 at 03.30, a specially trained strike force of 7 Camels launched an audacious attack across 75 miles of open sea to attack the Zeppelin sheds at Tondern. First to go was the Flight of Captains W. F. Dickson, W. D. Jackson and Lieutenant N. E. Williams. The next Flight consisted of Captains B. A. Smart and T. K. Thyne, and Lieutenants S. Dawson and W. A. Yeullett. Thyne's Camel developed engine trouble and he returned to the *Furious*.

The remaining 6 aircraft swept in low over the two sheds and dropped their twelve 50-lb bombs. Both sheds erupted in flames, destroying L54 and L60. Yeullett ran out of petrol and was drowned when his aircraft came down in the sea. Jackson, Williams and Dawson landed in neutral Denmark and were interned. Dickson and Smart returned to land in the sea close to the destroyer *Violent* and were picked up. It was the first and last carrier-launched raid of the war.

Despite this success, landing trials were far from satisfactory with even the experienced Rutland nearly losing his life. On 30 March 1918, a report was submitted by Rutland and Flight-Lieutenants W. D. Jackson and R. K. Thyne. It said that the danger of not making a central landing had been emphasized in the case of Thyne who was blown over the side before landing. The report said: "By building a flying-deck aft you deliberately create air bumps and eddies due to natural forces." Rutland recommended that *Furious* be fitted with a continuous flight-deck and she became a take-off carrier only, until going in for another refit in 1921.

The 9,800-ton cruiser HMS *Cavendish*, modified like the *Furious*, joined the Fleet in October 1918. With the end of the war and the general acceptance of the need for a continuous flush flight-deck, with an upperworks on the starboard side, she was placed in Reserve and operated as a catapult trials ship until 1927.

In the DH4, de Havilland produced one of the outstanding aircraft of the era. Although the first aircraft built specifically as a day bomber, it had as good a performance as many fighters then in service. It entered service with 2 Squadron in March, and 5 Squadron in April 1917, replacing the Strutters.

The former fighter squadrons 6 and 11 were re-equipped with them and 17 Squadron, formed on 13 January 1918, had them as their first aircraft. Its fighting qualities were demonstrated when Leckie (later AM Sir Robert) and Major Cadbury (later Sir Egbert), flying a DH4 from Great Yarmouth, shot down the L70 – then the finest Zeppelin built – on 5 August 1918.

Wing Captain Lambe, Dunkirk, compared the DH4 with the Large Americas and favoured them on many counts, not least that they were easy to manufacture and repair; could leave at a moment's notice; could fly in weather that made it impossible to get a seaplane off the water, and he concluded that if they could be fitted with flotation bags, the disadvantages of smaller radius of action disappeared. They could be fitted for long-distance patrols with extra petrol tanks and carry a 230-lb or 2 × 100-lb bombs for anti-submarine work.

When the RNAS and RFC merged on 1 April 1918 to form the RAF, the RNAS Squadrons were renumbered in the 200 series reserved for them – 1 Squadron became No. 201 and so on. The Wings had a 6 added before their previous number, so that No. 3 became No. 63 Wing. Most naval ranks disappeared to be replaced by their military equivalents:

Commodore: Brigadier
Wing Captain: Colonel
Wing Commander: Lieutenant-Colonel
Squadron Commander: Major
Flight Commander: Captain
Flight-Lieutenant: Lieutenant
Flight Sub-Lieutenant: 2nd Lieutenant
Chief Petty Officer 1st Grade: Sergeant-Major 1st Class

Rear-Admiral Mark Kerr, CB, became Deputy Chief of the Air Staff with rank as Major-General, RAF, and Godfrey Paine, CB, MO, Master General of Personnel in the rank of Major-General, RAF.

At about this time too, some important suggestions were put forward by Scarlett (DAD Naval Staff) on anti-submarine operations. He said that COs, pilots and observers were handicapped in hunting enemy submarines because they lacked knowledge and experience of them. As a result, the Admiralty printed a pamphlet containing all relevant information for crews employed on anti-submarine duties.

Scarlett was also responsible for suggestions that experiments be conducted with the more rugged seaplanes, able to land and take off in fairly rough sea conditions. His idea was to fit the seaplanes with a hydrophone for anti-submarine operations. They would work in pairs, one landing on the sea to operate the detection equipment and the other remaining in the air ready to bomb the submarine when found.

Senior Commands at 1 April 1918

Station	Use	In Command
Anglesey	airship	Flt Cdr M. C. Brotherton
Calshot	seaplane	Sqn Cdr T. H. England, DSC
Cattewater	seaplane	Sqn Cdr F. K. Haskins, DSC
Cherbourg	seaplane	Sqn Cdr H. E. Watkins
Chingford	school	Wg Cdr G. F. Kilner, DSO
Cranwell	school, depot, airship	Cdre J. Luce, CB, RN
Crystal Palace	depot	Act Cdr K. G. Brooke
Dover–Dunkirk:	general	Wg Capt C. L. Lambe, DSO, RN
No. 1 Wing St Pol	aeroplane	Wg Cdr P. M. Fellowes, DSO
No. 4 Wing La Panne	aeroplane	Act Wg Cdr E. Osmond
No. 5 Wing Couderkerque	aeroplane	Wg Cdr J. T. Cull, DSO
Attached RFC:		
No. 16	aeroplane	Sqn Cdr H. A. Buss, DSC
No. 3	aeroplane	Act Sqn Cdr R. Collishaw
Nos 5, 11, 14 and 15	aeroplane	
Dover	aeroplane/seaplane	Act Wg Cdr F. K. McClean
Dundee	seaplane	Sqn Cdr E. S. Wilberforce
Eastbourne	school	Sqn Cdr F. B. Fowler
Eastchurch	school	Capt J. M. Steel, RN
East Fortune	school, airship	Wg Capt R. C. S. Hunt
Felixstowe	general	Wg Cdr J. C. Porte
Grain:	seaplane	Wg Cdr H. R. Busteed
	armament	Sqn Cdr R. A. Chalmers
	test flight	Wg Cdr J. L. Travers
Howden	airship	Wg Cdr Hon C. M. P. Brabazon
Killingholme	general	Wg Cdr C. R. Finch-Noyes
Lee-On-Solent	school	Sqn Cdr D. S. Evill, DSC
Longside	airship	Sqn Cdr R. S. Robinson
Luce Bay	airship	Sqn Cdr L. H. Hartford
Malta	seaplane	Wg Cdr H. M. Cave-Brown-Cave
Manston	general	Wg Capt H. P. Smyth Osbourne
	war school	Sqn Cdr L. S. Breadner, DSC
	DH4 school	Sqn Cdr E. T. Newton-Clare, DSO
	school	Sqn Cdr R. H. Jones
Mudros	general	Act Wg Capt R. Gordon, DSO
Mullion	general	Sqn Cdr R. B. Colmore
Orkney	Division	Wg Capt O. Swann
Otranto No. 6 Wing	seaplane	Wg Cdr C. H. K. Edmonds, DSO
Pembroke	airship	Sqn Cdr R. C. Hayes
Polegate	airship	Sqn Cdr I. Fraser
Portsmouth	Group	Wg Cdr A. W. Bigsworth, DSO
Pulham	airship	Wg Cdr F. L. N. Boothby
Rosyth	base	Act Wg Cdr I. G. V. Fowler
Scillies	seaplane	Flt Cdr R. B. Maycock
South Shields	depot	Sqn Cdr W. G. Sitwell
S.W. Group	general	Wg Capt E. L. Gerrard, DSO
Stonehenge	HP Sqn	Act Wg Cdr J. T. Babington, DSO
Strathbeg	seaplane	Wg Cdr R. P. Ross, DSO
Tregantle and Withnoe	depot	RA. J. de M. Hutchison, CVO, CMG
Torquay	seaplane	Sqn Cdr K. C. Buss
Vendôme	school	Wg Cdr E. T. R. Chambers
Yarmouth	general	Wg Capt C. R. Samson, DSO

Carriers

Campania, City of Oxford, Empress, Engadine, Furious, Manxman, Nairana, Pegasus, Riviera, Vindex. **Wg Cdr C. E. Risk** was in charge of carriers, Port Said.

Ship's Aircraft

HMS *Furious* had 6 Ship's Camels with BR1 engines, numbered N6767, 6777, 6815, 6825, 6832, 6840; and 15 Ship Strutters W/T with 130 Clerget engines, numbered A5951, 5997, 5999, 6000, 6019, 6911, 6913, 6917, 6972, 6985, 6987, 6988, 6989, 6990, and B744.

HMS *Campania* had 7 Strutter W/T, 9722 with 110 Clerget and the rest with 130 Clerget numbered N5633, 5638, A6919, 6920, 6921, 6922, and one Strutter N5635.
There were 4 Campania W/T Seaplanes, numbered N1842, 1850, 2372 (Eagle 8 engine); N2366 (Eagle 4), and Campania N2375 (Eagle 8).
HMS *Nairana* had 5 Campania W/T (Eagle 8) numbered N1844, 1847, 1848, 1849, 2370; and 2 Sopwith Baby with 130 Clerget, N1440, 1441.
HMS *Pegasus* had 4 Ship's Camel 150 BR1, N6788, 6820, 6826, 6836; 3 Campania W/T N1851, 2369 (Eagle 8), N2364 (Eagle 4) and a Short 184 (Maori) N9069.
HMS *Vindictive* had a Griffin with B2 engine, N100.
HMS *Vindex* (No. 15 Group, Mudros) had 5 Short 184, numbers N1750, 2633, 2814, and W/T type N2634, 2813.
HMS *Ark Royal* had 3 Hamble Baby, N1476, 1984, 1985; one Short 184, N1786, and 2 Sopwith Baby, N1424 and W/T N2074.
HMS *Riviera* (No. 6 Group, Taranto) had Short 184, N2929, 2930, 2943, 2948.
HMS *Manxman* (Malta) had 3 Ship's Camel, N6806, 6807, 6808.
HMS *City of Oxford* (No. 64 Wing, Alexandria) had a Short 827 W/T N8469.
HMS *Engadine* (Gibraltar Group) had 3 Short 184, N2916 W/T, 2944, 2945.

Type and engine	Number	HMS
Camel 150 B.R.1	N6603	*Tiger*
	6614	*Indomitable*
	6758	*Princess Royal*
	6778	*Penelope*
	6790	*Australia*
	6792	*Inflexible*
	6793	*Courageous*
	6794	*Melbourne*
	6811	*Comus*
	6816	*Aurora*
	6817	*Inflexible*
	6822	*Sydney*
	6824	*Undaunted*
	6828	*Dublin*
	6831	*Royalist*
	6833	*New Zealand*
	6838	*Renown*
	6848	*Chatham*
	6849	*Princess Royal*
	7106	*Repulse*
	7110	*Penelope*
	7111	*Birkenhead*
	7112	*Southampton*
	7116	*Galatea*
	7117	*Glorious*
	7119	*Inconstant*
	7121	*Caroline*
	7122	*Casandra*
Strutter W/T 130 Clerget	A5998	*Courageous*
	6905	*Glorious*
	6966	*Indomitable*
	6968	*Australia*
	6980	*Inflexible*
	F2215	*Renown*
	2220	*New Zealand*
	2224	*Repulse*

On 30 September 1918 the machines on naval flying duties with the Grand Fleet or in the Mediterranean were made up as follows:

Aeroplanes	Total
BE2C	10
DH4	29

DH6	5
DH9	128
Hamble Convert	3
H. Farman	5
Snipe	2
Sopwith Strutter 2-seater	54
Sopwith Strutter	4
Sopwith Strutter converted to ship use	57
Sopwith Pup	11
Sopwith Camel	173

Seaplanes and Ship Aeroplanes

ADF Boat	20
Campania	46
Fairey 3A/B/C	58
FBA	36
Hamble Baby	18
Large America H12	12
Large America H12 Convert	6
Large America H16	65
Small America	2
F2A	48
F3	87
NT 2B	58
Panther	2
Porte Boat	2
Short 827	4
Short 184	292
Short 166	2
Short 320	59
SB3D	56
Ship's Camel	133
Shirl	2
Sopwith T1	53
Sopwith Baby	64
Wight	12
Experimental/miscellaneous	25

Mediterranean District, No. 15 Group, Mudros

Aeroplanes
  1 BE2C
  3 BE2E (2 × W/T)
14 DH4 (8 × W/T)
  4 DH6
30 DH9 (1 × W/T)
  4 HF Trop
  5 Sopwith Pups
  2 Sopwith Bombers
55 Sopwith Camels

Seaplanes
  1 HF Trop
  4 Hamble Baby
  1 Short 166
30 Short 184 (23 × W/T)
  5 Sopwith Baby (1 × W/T)

Aeroplanes
10 DH4   **No. 6 Group, Taranto**
32 DH9
  3 Hamble Converts
16 Short 320 (2 × W/T)
  1 Sopwith Baby

Seaplanes	2 F3 (1 × W/T)	**Otranto**
	1 Hamble Baby	
	5 Short 184 (3 × W/T)	
	16 Short 320 (2 × W/T)	
	1 Sopwith Baby	
	1 Hamble Baby	**St Maria de Leuca**
	1 Short 184 (W/T)	
	1 Short 320	
	3 Sopwith Baby	
Aeroplanes	2 DH9 (W/T)	**Malta**
	2 Sopwith Camels	
Seaplanes	3 Ship Camels	
	4 Short 184 (W/T)	
	1 F3	**No. 64 Wing, Alexandria**
	8 Short 184 (7 × W/T)	
	2 Sopwith Baby	
	1 Hamble Baby	**Port Said**
	2 Short 184 single	
	9 Short 184 (8 × W/T)	
	2 Sopwith Baby	

APPROXIMATE STRENGTH 1914–1918 (Aeroplanes and seaplanes combined)

Date		Machines	Officers	Men	Total
2 Aug	1914	93	138	589	727
Dec	1914	181	476	3,769	4,245
	1915	1,030	1,634	11,041	12,675
	1916	1,599	2,764	26,129	28,893
	1917	2,851	4,765	43,050	47,815
To RAF 1 April 1918		2,949	5,378	49,688	55,066

During 1919, the rundown of ex-RNAS bases at home and abroad continued with a rapidity which becomes inevitable in peacetime.

Stations	Date
Pembroke	14 January 1919
Bangor	22 January 1919
Newly, Prawle Point and Westward Ho!	22 February 1919
Bembridge	5 May 1919
Felixstowe, Fishguard	10 May 1919
Calshot, Cattewater, Dover, Newhaven, Torquay and Tresco	15 May 1919
Portland	18 June 1919
Tynemouth, Hornsea and Dundee	30 June 1919
Killingholme	8 October 1919
Great Yarmouth	31 December 1919
Westgate	7 February 1920

Overseas Bases	
Mudros, Otranto	9 December 1918
Alexandria, Basra and Cherbourg	15 March 1919
Dunkirk and Malta	1 September 1919
Port Said	15 November 1919

SEAPLANE CONTRACTS PLACED

Type	Maker	Numbers	Total Ordered	Delivered
Panther	Parnall	N7400–7459	150	
		N7680–7841	162	
Ship's Camel	Beardmore	N7350–7399	50	
		N7650–7679	30	
	Pegler	N7100–7149	50	39
	Sage	N7300–7349	50	
Shirl	Blackburn	N7850–7979	130	
Sopwith T1	Blackburn	N7550–7649	100	
		N6950–6999	50	40
		N6900–6929	30	4
		N7980–8079	100	
	Fairfield	N7000–7099	100	13
	Pegler	N6930–6949	20	
Fairey 3B	Fairey	N2230–2259	30	11
		N9230–9259	30	
Short 184	Brush	N9060–9099	40	27
		N9260–9289	30	
		N9350–9399	50	
	Robey	N9000–9059	60	39
		N9140–9169	30	
		N9290–9349	60	
	Supermarine	N9170–9199	30	3
	J. S. White	N2950–2999	50	47
		N9100–9139	40	
		N9400–9449	50	
H16	Curtiss	N4060–4074	15	14
F2A	Aircraft	N4890–4949	60	59
		N4480–4504	25	2
	May, Harden & May	N4560–4579	20	
	Saunders	N4080–4099	20	6
F3	Dick Kerr	N4430–4479	50	
		N4230–4279	50	41
	Phoenix	N4100–4117	18	
		N4160–4179	20	5
		N4400–4429	30	
	Short	N4180–4183	4	
	Malta Yard	N4000–4035	36	9
F5 (Liberty)	Dick Kerr	N4360–4397	38	3
F5	Dick Kerr	N4730–4779	50	
	Gosport Co.	N4118–4149	32	
	May, Harden & May	N4630–4670	50	
	Phoenix	N4680–4729	50	
		N4780–4829	50	
	Saunders	N4184–4229	46	
	Short	N4580–4629	50	
		N4036–4049	14	
ADF Boat	Supermarine	N4830–4879	50	
NT 2B	Saunders	N2450–2455	6	5
	Supermarine	N2500–2523	24	2
		N2760–2784	25	19
	N. Thompson	N3300–3374	75	
		N2400–2429	30	21
		N2260–2359	100	

There was a total of 2,134 seaplanes and ship aeroplanes still on order.

BETWEEN THE WARS

In May 1918, DAD sent a memo to ACA suggesting that with some former seaplane carriers operating landplanes as well, the term Aircraft Carrier should be used for them. This memo was forwarded to Major-General Sykes who had succeeded Trenchard as Chief of the Air Staff, and appears to be the first time these words were used. Later in the year, DAD was also instrumental in pointing out, again for the first time, the urgent need for an Anti-Submarine Warfare School.

On 30 August, HMS *Argus* began a series of flying-on trials with Sopwith Strutters, flown by Lt-Colonel R. Bell Davies, VC, and Captain L. H. Cockey from Turnhouse. In view of the difficulties experienced in the *Furious*, *Argus* was designed with a flush flight-deck with funnel gases expelled by fans through horizontal smoke ducts opening up aft. The chart house was raised or lowered by lifts and two wireless masts were hinged to fall flush with the deck. Twenty aircraft could be stowed in the hangar which was divided into four sections by fireproof screens. There were two lifts to range aircraft on deck. The hull contained adequate workshops, torpedo and bomb stores. Davies had moved from the *Campania* to the *Furious* as Senior Flying Officer, with Lt-Colonel R. H. Clark-Hall (former CO of *Ark Royal*) as ACA's Staff Officer. The *Argus* had a flight-deck 550 ft (168 m) long with a beam of 68 ft (21 m) and for these trials, Davies was in command of the RAF contingent in the *Argus*.

Captain Nicholson (*Furious*) was convinced that it was necessary to hold aircraft steady after landing on and suggested an overlapping row of hooks fitted to the undercarriage, to engage fore and aft wires supported between two ramps about 30 ft apart. The ramps sloped upwards from aft to bows to a height of about 2 ft. The idea was that the aircraft would land on, run up and over the first ramp, before dropping into the trap and being arrested.

Davies reported that at first it was not easy to land close to the ship's stern, but although aircraft often landed on with drift and off the centre line, it was easy to straighten them up. The best place for the landing gear was as far forward as possible.

The second landing trials took place on 26 September, after which the ship entered dockyard hands for the ramps to be fitted. On 1 October 1918, three landings were made and the aircraft were satisfactorily held between the ramps, with the hooks engaging all the wires caught. These landings were by far the most successful that had yet taken place.

On 4 December, the Admiralty held a conference at which DAD, then Brigadier-General R. M. Groves, put forward proposals for post-war naval aviation. The *Furious*, *Vindictive*, *Argus*, *Pegasus*, *Nairana* and *Vindex* were to be retained, with the *Eagle* and *Hermes* completing in 1919. It was recommended that all fully manned light cruisers should carry one aeroplane, with battleships and battle-cruisers carrying two.

The Sopwith Cuckoo was the first torpedo-bomber landplane capable of operating from a carrier. The first batch went to the Torpedo Training School at East Fortune on 7 October 1918, and the first operational squadron joined the *Argus* on 19 October, with 18 aircraft. Originally powered by a 200-hp Hispano Suiza, they had a top speed of 103 mph (90 knots), were 28.5 ft long (9 m), a span of 46 ft 9 ins (14 m), a service ceiling of 12,100 ft (3,689 m) and an endurance of 4 hours. They were armed with a Mk1X 18-inch torpedo below the fuselage. The original engines proved unsatisfactory, and these were eventually replaced with Sunbeam Arabs. The Mk2 version had a Wolseley Viper. The Armistice came before the Cuckoos could be used in action when 90 had been delivered and 350 were on order. The aircraft proved ideal for carrier operations and remained in service until April 1923, when No. 210 Squadron disbanded at Gosport.

Without the impetus of war, progress was very slow and many experienced observers felt that the Admiralty was only too pleased to be rid of their 'problem child' for which they were unable to see an economically viable role. The White Paper of 1919 did attempt to define the functions of the RAF, but although the Navy and Army undoubtably believed that separate squadrons would be attached to them, under their control, this was firmly resisted by the Air Ministry. This White Paper (Cmnd 467) mentioned almost as an aside, "... within the framework of the RAF ... there will be a small part of it trained for work with the Royal Navy."

As a result of the successful trials in the *Argus*, work was allowed to proceed on the 10,850-ton *Hermes* and the former Chilean battleship *Almirante Cochrane*, renamed HMS *Eagle*. *Hermes* was the first ship in the world specifically designed as a carrier and was launched at Elswick in 1919 and towed to Devonport for completion. The design was a compromise solution to carrier problems with a medium sized, fairly fast ship with a wide radius of action, relying on screening warships for defence. The *Eagle* completed her preliminary trials in 1920 and was transferred to Portsmouth for completion (bottom photograph).

As heavier aircraft entered service, the greater weight and higher landing-on speeds resulted in damage to undercarriages, and the percentage of write-offs continued to increase.

By the time they were ready for operations, the 'Flying Squadron' of the *Furious*, *Argus*, *Nairana*, *Pegasus*, *Vindex* and *Vindictive* had rapidly disappeared with only the *Argus* left in home waters. The seaplane carrier *Ark Royal* was overseas.

The Air Estimates for 1920 only allowed for 25½ squadrons and of these, one was allowed for naval bases and 2½ for the Home Fleet. On one point the Admiralty did win the day. All aircraft flown off HM ships and all air operations over the sea remained under their control. The general procedure was for the Admiralty to formulate its requirements and for the RAF to embark the necessary squadrons and personnel.

During 1924–1925, the fore and aft arrester wire system was abandoned and until the transverse system was perfected for operational use in 1933, aircraft relied on the lowest possible approach speeds and the highest possible wind speed over the deck, to halt them. To minimize the risk of going over the side, wire palisades were erected on either side of the flight-deck.

Up to 1924, the authorized strength of the Navy was 12 Flights totalling 78 aircraft. There was an urgent need for expansion if we were to retain our position as a leading naval air power. Admiral Chatfield had already recommended that two battle-cruisers – *Courageous* and *Glorious* – should be converted to carriers. Resulting from modifications to the Treaty of Washington, these plans were pressed forward. The *Glorious* converted at Rosyth and Devonport 1924–1930, and the *Courageous* at Devonport 1924–1928.

During this period, senior appointments in carriers were held by RAF officers and this stopped the Navy building up a nucleus of officers trained in aviation. Proposals that NOs take temporary commissions in the RAF to gain flying experience met with a cold response. Even in RAF Coastal Area where personal friendly relations had been established between Air Commodore Samson, COS, and Bell Davies, Head of Naval Air, an Air Ministry interpretation of correct procedure finally broke that link with their insistence that all approaches should be made through the Air Council.

One other major question worried naval experts. The small number of direct entry observers had returned to civilian life. The only trained ones were ex-Yeoman-of-Signals, trained in the old *Campania*. They had transferred to the RAF as 2nd lieutenants and most were now flying officers. Skilled observers were essential and not enough progress was being made with air-spotting for the Navy.

The Navy's first big step forward followed the Beatty recommendations which resulted in a special sub-committee of the

CID presenting a report in 1924. This stated that all Fleet reconnaissance and air-spotting duties should be performed by NOs. In April 1924 came another major breakthrough when the FAA of the RAF was formed. The agreement provided that 70% of all naval pilots should be RN or RM officers, and allowed the majority of RAF personnel in carriers to be replaced by naval ratings. The name Fleet Air Arm was ruled to apply only to those units embarked in carriers.

Although the Air Ministry remained responsible for aircraft production, the Admiralty specified numbers and type, and paid the bill. There is little to suggest that at this time the Admiralty were worried about the situation. Although they created the post of Flag Officer (Air), with RA R. G. Henderson as the first holder, in March 1931, funds only allowed for the addition of 18 aircraft.

By October 1924, aircraft strength had increased slightly to 18 Flights of 128 aircraft. During 1925 the *Furious* completed her refit and entered service with up to 36 aircraft, and the following year on 7 July, piloting a Blackburn Dart TB, Flight-Lieutenant G. H. Boyce made the first night landing on the *Furious*. Contemporary aircraft were the Blackburn Blackburn and Avro Bison. All were biplanes and suffered from the design problems then inherent with carrier aircraft, and their performance was poor compared with landplane standards. The front-line fighter was the Fairey Flycatcher

The famous Flycatcher was a superb aerobatic biplane, delightful to fly, easy to land on a carrier and had a full throttle roar which delighted any onlookers. A feature shared with other famous Fairey aircraft of the time such as the 3F, was the patented camber-changing mechanism on the wings and flaps which ran along the trailing edges of both wings, with the outer sections lowered for landing and take-off. From about 1923–1934, it was the standard single-seat fighter of the Navy and until the first Nimrods entered service, was the only Fleet Fighter. It was the last fighter to be used for catapult take-offs from the gun turrets of capital ships.

The Flycatcher did service trials in HMS *Argus* during February 1923 and was equipped with 'steel jaws' on the undercarriage spreader bars to engage the typical fore and aft arrester wires – a system abandoned in 1926. The Flycatcher was the first FAA aircraft fitted with hydraulic wheel brakes which could reduce a landing run to 50 yards.

They first entered service with 402 Flight in 1923, and in 1924 they replaced the Nieuport Nightjars and Parnall Plovers in 403 and 404 Flights. Two new units, 405 and 406 Flights, were similarly equipped during 1924–1925 and in 1933, with the formation of Squadrons from Flights, they equipped 801 until superseded by Ospreys and Nimrods.

The *Courageous* as converted had a single funnel on the starboard side, rising up through a narrow superstructure which carried the navigation position, searchlights, flying control, and a light signal mast. They were armed with sixteen 4.7-inch AA guns, and although these may seem rather light compared to the 8-inch of the US and Japanese cruisers – the maximum size permitted under the Treaty of Washington – the Admiralty rightly considered they should avoid action with capital ships at all costs and rely on screening ships to protect them from cruiser attack. During a further refit 1934–1936, the quarter-deck was raised to the level of the upper deck, to secure dryness aft.

Displacing 22,500 ton, the *Courageous* was 786 ft long (240 m), with a beam of 81 ft (25 m), and 90,000-shp geared turbines gave her a speed of 31 knots. She was designed to carry 48 aircraft. Her flight-deck was 570 ft (174 m) long, with a beam of 110 ft (33 m).

On 26 November 1929, a Flycatcher from Malta made the first ever night deck-landing by a fighter in HMS *Courageous*. This carrier, and her sister ships *Furious* and *Glorious*, operated Flycatchers 'slip flights' from a 60-ft (18 m) tapered runway which led from their hangar below the main flight-deck It was common for them to drop out of sight below the bows before gaining height. The aircraft was phased out in 1935.

The Flycatcher was a single-seat fighter with a composite wood/metal frame, fabric covered, built by the Fairey Aviation Company, Hayes. Powered by an Armstrong Siddeley 400-hp Jaguar 3 or 4, it had a top speed of 133 mph (116 knots) at 5,000 ft (1,525 m); a service ceiling of 19,000 ft (5,793 m); a span of 29 ft (8.8 m); a length of 23 ft (7 m); and a height of 12 ft (3.7 m). It was armed with two Vickers machine-guns and could carry four 20-lb (9 kg) bombs below the wings. Cruising range was about 315 miles (504 km).

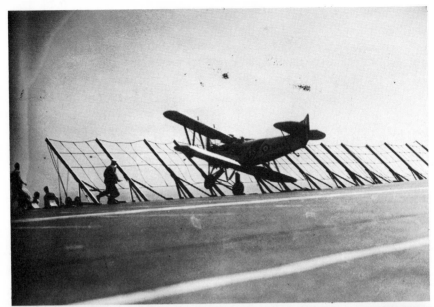

In these early days and throughout the Second World War, until the
duties were taken over by SAR helicopters, a carrier was always
accompanied by a destroyer, whose duty was to act as plane guard and
hope to rescue any crews unfortunate enough to ditch. Sometimes,

despite a pitching deck and a bad landing, the wire palisades were sufficient to stop an aircraft going over the side. Others were not so lucky. This sequence shows an aircraft turning upside down as it goes over the side, and the guard destroyer hurrying to the rescue.

Entering service at about the same time as the Flycatcher was the Supermarine Seagull III, first seen at Hendon in 1922. Fuel tanks were under the top mainplane centre section and it was the first single-engined flying boat to use gravity feed. It was from this and subsequent designs that the Seagull V – later renamed the Walrus – came. No. 440 FR Flight was first equipped with the Seagull in 1923; between 1924 and 1931 No 440 was in HMS *Eagle*, mainly in the Mediterranean. Powered by a 450-hp Napier Lion, it had a maximum speed of 108 mph (94 knots) at sea level, climbed to 5,000 ft (1,524 m) in five minutes, and was armed with one Lewis gun amidships. Span was 46 ft (14 m), length 37 ft (11 m), and height 12 ft (3.6 m). Loaded weight was 5,668 lb (1,728 kg).

The Seagulls were eventually replaced with Fairey IIIDs, and the spotter amphibian as a type disappeared until the Walrus came along in 1933. A Seagull III amphibian and a Fairey IIIF floatplane are shown below.

The Fairey IIIF was the last of this series which started in 1917, and some 620 were built for the RAF and their FAA. The prototype flew on 19 March 1926 and was designed for a crew of 3 with a TAG (telegraphist air gunner) and had a distinctive tall rudder. The type did deck-landing trials in the *Furious* in 1927, the same year the first air-operated catapult was installed in HMS *Frobisher*.

The IIIF entered service with No. 440 Flight in 1928, and remained in service with the Navy until 1936. It had no arrester hook, although one was fitted with the triangular steel-framed deck hook operated by the pilot for trials in the *Courageous* during 1931. This type of arrester hook was later fitted to the Osprey, following the final trials with transverse arrester wires.

Powered by a Napier Lion of 570-hp, it had a maximum speed of 120 mph (104 knots), a span of 45 ft 9 in (14 m), a length of 34 – 36 ft (10 – 11 m), a height of 14 ft 2 in (4 m), and an endurance of 4 hours. Service ceiling was 20,000 ft (6,098 m). Armed with a fixed Vickers gun forward and a Lewis gun on a Scarff mounting for the rear cockpit, it could carry up to 500 lb of bombs (227 kg) below the wings. Slow rate of climb, 6 minutes to 5,000 ft (1524 m).

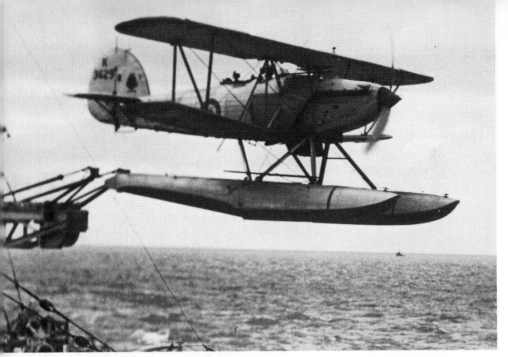

The Hawker Osprey was the first of a new type of aircraft for the FAA, the fast two-seater, fighter reconnaissance type which was developed from the RAF's Hart. The naval variant had folding wings, and flotation gear, and the Mk1s first equipped Nos 404 and 409 Flights in November 1932 and from 1933, when the squadrons were first formed, they joined the Nimrods in 800, 801 and 802 Squadrons. In late 1938, 803 Squadron embarked their Ospreys in the new *Ark Royal* for its shake-down and working-up trials. They remained in service until replaced by the Skuas in 1939. The seaplane version, like the Mk3 shown above, catapulted from HMS *Sussex*, replaced the Fairey IIIFs of 407 Flight, 2nd Cruiser Squadron, Home Fleet. Powered by a 640-hp Rolls-Royce Kestrel, it had a maximum speed of 176 mph (153 knots) – seaplane version 169 mph (147 knots), an endurance of 2½ hours, service ceiling of 22,000 ft (6,707 m), climb 1,300 ft/min (396 m/min), and was armed with a fixed Vickers and a free-mounted Lewis gun. Span was 37 ft down to 15 ft 7 in folded (11 m to 4.8 m), length 29 ft 4 in (9 m), and height 10 ft 5 in (3.2 m) (seaplane 12 ft 5 in – 3.8 m).

The Nimrod, right, was a variant of the RAF's Fury and was a replacement for the Flycatcher. A prototype flew in 1930 and the production Mk1 first flew on 20 September 1931. It had no arrester gear. It was superseded by the Mk2 with arrester gear and Nimrods replaced the Flycatchers of Nos 402, 408, and 409 Flights and later 800, 801 and 802 Squadrons, from 1932 onwards.

100

Powered by a 590-hp Rolls-Royce Kestrel, maximum speed was 195 mph (170 knots), initial climb 1,640 ft/min (500 m/min), and ceiling 26,000 ft (7,927 m). Span was 33 ft 6 in (10 m), length 27 ft (8 m), and height 9 ft 9 in (3 m). Armed with twin Vickers synchronized machine-guns, it could carry four 20-lb (9 kg) bombs below wings.

By 1931, a series of Admiralty Fleet Orders (AFOs) had built up the FAA with its unique organization. A quarter of the pilots were RAF with the remainder being RN or RM officers holding temporary commissions in the RAF.

The first squadrons were formed in the April 1933 re-organization

with Nos 402 and 404 Flights becoming 800 Squadron with 12 aircraft in HMS *Courageous*. Flight No. 401 was brought up to strength by absorbing half of No. 404 Flight and became 801 Squadron with 9 aircraft in HMS *Furious*. Fighter squadrons were numbered in the 800s, FSR in the 810s and TSR in the 820s. Aircraft also carried distinguishing colour bands – *Courageous* red, *Glorious* yellow, *Eagle* green and *Hermes* black.

Of our carriers the *Argus* had withdrawn to Reserve, and the refit of the *Eagle* had been completed so that she could relieve the *Hermes* on the China Station, and *Hermes* could be refitted.

Lord Chatfield and the First Lord Samuel Hoare, pressed the case for Admiralty control to be re-opened and met formidable opposition

101

from Trenchard. Formal demands for the training of naval ratings as pilots, combined with the revision of terms under which RAF officers served with the Fleet, were made in 1935 and again in 1936.

The Navy Estimates of 1936 gave the FAA just over £3 million, and at the beginning of 1936 the disposition of aircraft in the Fleet was: *Courageous*: 3 Osprey, 9 Nimrod, 12 Baffin, 12 Seal, and 811 and 822 Squadron Swordfish – a total of 48 aircraft; *Furious*: 3 Osprey, 6 Nimrod, 12 Baffin, 12 Fairey IIIF – a total of 33 aircraft; *Eagle* in Reserve: 6 Osprey; *Hermes* China Station: 9 Seal; *Glorious*: 3 Osprey, 9 Nimrod, 12 Seal, 12 Baffin, 12 Fairey IIIF – a total of 48 aircraft. This was a total of 144 aircraft, and in addition 29 ships of the Fleet were fitted with catapults and carried 34 aircraft.

By March 1937 the Admiralty was slowly winning the battle and Churchill – converted to the Unified Air Force idea after he first left office – returned to the naval fold with all his old verve and enthusiasm. Finally, in July, the Admiralty gained official approval to take over the administrative and operational control of naval flying. Although it did not gain control of Coastal Command, it was stated on 1 December 1937 that in time of war Coastal Command would provide trade protection and co-operate with the RN.

The Naval Air Branch, consisting of officers entered for air duties only, was instituted on 17 February 1937. It was also agreed that the Air Branch would have its own shore establishments and aerodromes to accommodate personnel disembarked ashore.

The post of Assistant Chief of Naval Staff (Air) was created and the first holder was Rear-Admiral J. D. Cunningham. In January 1938, two new departments were formed at the Admiralty, Air Materiel and Air Personnel. On 18 November 1938, the Air Branch of the RNVR was formed and the first four aerodromes handed over – Lee-on-Solent, Worthy Down, Ford and Donibristle. The first Flag Officer Naval Air Stations (Lee-on-Solent) was Rear-Admiral R. Bell Davies, VC, one of the few pioneer air pilots to remain with the RN. For the first time too, a Captain (E) was appointed as technical adviser.

HMS *Argus* was recommissioned on 9 August 1937 as parent ship for the RAF Queen Bee Flight and for training in deck-landing. The disposition at the end of 1938 was: the *Ark Royal* – 800 and 803 (F), 814, 820, 821 (TSR). *Hermes* officers under training, Queen Bee Flight and one FRU. *Glorious* in the Mediterranean had 802 (F), 818, 823 and 825 (TSR). By 1939, there were seven carriers operating a total of 220 aircraft with the Blackburn Skua – a monoplane introduced for the first time as a dive bomber – equipping two squadrons in the *Ark Royal*.

It was not, however, until 28 May 1939 that the Admiralty finally

102

took over control and the Fleet Air Arm was established. With the loss of so many experienced naval aviators to the RAF in 1918, the Navy had few men with the experience necessary to take over Command or Staff appointments, and they had to lean heavily on the Air Staff when drafting staff requirements and accepting design tenders based on specifications drawn up by the Air Staff. Although orders had been placed for four new armoured carriers, of the Illustrious Class, and two more had been ordered in 1938, the first was unlikely to enter service until 1940.

The Walrus Vickers Supermarine Seagull amphibian with a Bristol Pegasus pusher-mounted engine was about to join the Fleet. Known as the Walrus, it was the first British military aircraft with a fully retractable undercarriage; first in the world to be catapulted from a warship with a full military load, and the first FAA machine with a fully enclosed cockpit. The Walrus or 'Shagbat' as it was affectionately known, did sterling work with the Fleet until 1944, when it was supplemented by the Sea Otter.

What is perhaps not so well known is that the prototype which flew on 21 June 1933 was designed by the famous designer of the Spitfire, Mr R. J. Mitchell. The first Air Ministry Contract was in May 1935 and after 280 had been built by Supermarine, production went to Saunders-Roe so that Supermarine could concentrate on the Spitfire.

Powered by a Bristol Pegasus of 775-hp, it had a span of 45 ft 10 in (14 m), 17 ft 11 in folded (5.5 m), a length of 37 ft 3 in (11 m), and a height of 15 ft 3 in (4.5 m). Loaded weight was 7,200 lb (3,273 kg).

THE WAR YEARS AND BEYOND

There were enough aircrews for the existing squadrons in 1939, but the expanding needs of new units and second line duties, coupled with the losses during the Norwegian Campaign and the Dunkirk operations, led to a real dilution of skill and experience. This was to rob the FAA of success on a number of occasions during the early years of the Second World War.

Few aircrews were more than partly trained in A/S warfare and escort carriers were still a dream of the future. The *Courageous* and the *Ark Royal* were sent to operate north and south-west of Ireland, and on 14 September the *Ark Royal* was attacked by U39 whose two torpedoes narrowly missed their target. On 17 September, the *Courageous* was torpedoed and sunk by U29 with heavy loss of life. This first major naval loss together with the near miss on the *Ark Royal* led to Fleet carriers being withdrawn from A/S duties.

The Swordfish Saga started at the outbreak of war when this amazing aircraft equipped 14 squadrons. In the *Ark Royal*: 810, 814, 820, 821; *Courageous*: 811, 822; *Eagle*: 813, 824; *Glorious*: 823, 825; *Furious*: 816, 818, 701, 702 Catapult Flights for the Fleet.

The 'Stringbag', as the Swordfish was known, always remains a vivid memory for me. I first flew in it from HMS *Courageous* in late 1938. It was my first flight in any aircraft and as we took off with a 40-knot wind over deck, I shall never forget my amazement as the carrier passed beneath us.

The TSR1 first flew at Fairey's Great West Aerodrome (now Heathrow Airport) on 21 March 1933 and production aircraft had a standard Bristol Pegasus engine of 690-hp, giving a maximum speed of 140 mph (224 km/h). It carried a variety of weapons, including the 18-inch 1,610-lb (732 kg) torpedo, and had a synchronized Vickers machine-gun firing forward and a free-mounted one aft. The later Swordfish 2 could carry eight 60-lb rockets beneath the wings, and on 23 May 1943 Sub-Lieutenant H. Horrocks, 819 Squadron in HMS *Archer*, sank U-752 west of Ireland, the first success with this new operational weapon.

The Swordfish will for ever be linked with the names of HMS *Ark Royal*, and Lieutenant-Commanders Eugene Esmonde and T. P. Coode; the attacks on *Gneisenau, Tirpitz, Prinz Eugen*, and *Bismarck*; and – perhaps the outstanding achievement – the Taranto Raid by 816, 819 Squadrons (*Illustrious*), and 813, 824 Squadrons (*Eagle*) embarked in *Illustrious*. This devastating attack on 11

November 1940 severely damaged three battleships, a cruiser and auxiliary vessels, as well as oil installations and seaplane hangars.

Nine years after the first Swordfish joined an operational squadron, in the Spring of 1945, the aircraft still equipped nine front-line squadrons. Finally, on 21 May 1945, 836 Squadron – an operational pool MAC ships unit – disbanded. The last operational flight of a Swordfish was from the MAC *Empire Mackay*, 28 June 1945.

A TSR with 3 crew for reconnaissance or 2 crew for strikes, the Swordfish was 36 ft 4 in long (11 m), span 45 ft 6 in (13.9 m), and 12 ft 10 in high (3.94 m). Loaded weight was 9,250 lb (4,205 kg); it could climb to 5,000 ft (1,525 m) in 10 minutes, and had an operational range of 550 miles (880 km).

The Albacore (above) was intended to replace the Swordfish, but in the end was outlived by the older aircaraft. The Albacore set new standards in crew comfort with the enclosed cockpits being heated, the fitting of windscreen wipers and automatic launch of dinghy. There was an all-metal monocoque fuselage for the first time and the engine had a variable pitch propeller for rapid take-off and maximum cruising range. On 15 March 1940 826 Squadrons (Ford) was equipped with the aircraft and for a long period they were used mainly for shore-based operations.

On 26 November 1940, 826 and 829 Squadrons embarked in the *Formidable* which escorted a convoy to Cape Town. From 1943, Albacore squadrons re-equipped with Barracudas. Powered by a 1,065-hp Bristol Taurus, they had a maximum speed of 161 mph (140 knots), a climb of 750 ft/min (229 m/min) with a 2,000-lb (910 kg) load, and a range of 725 miles (1,160 km). Service ceiling was 20,700 ft (6,311 m). All-up weight with a full load of one 18-inch torpedo (1,610 lb–732 kg) or four 500-lb (227 kg) bombs, was 12,600 lb (5,727 kg). Armed with Vickers gun firing forward in starboard wing and twin Vickers rear cockpit. Span was 50 ft (15 m), length 39 ft 9 in (12 m), and height 15 ft 3 in (4.6 m).

Another 'crash landing' on the *Courageous*.

Commander Cedric Coxon, MVO, retired in April 1971 after 32 years as a naval pilot and was the last pilot still in flying practice to have flown the Swordfish during the war. Operating from Malta 1941–42, he made eight torpedo attacks against supply ships and sank five. His last flight was at the controls of the last Swordfish still operational at the 50th anniversary celebrations of A & AEE, Boscombe Down.

The Fairey Fulmar was the first Fairey fighter to be used by the FAA since the famous Flycatcher, and was the only fighter in the Navy with the same fire power as the Spitfire and Hurricane. The first eight-gun fighter with the FAA, the prototype flew on 13 January 1937 and the Mk2 entered service with 808 Squadron, Worthy Down, in June 1940 and later embarked in the *Ark Royal*. On 1 December 1940, three from 807 Squadron joined the *Pegasus* as the first to be used for the Catapult Fighter Ships.

805 Squadron, formed 1 January 1941 at Dekheila, Egypt, was the first to serve from a RNAS overseas. The last to form with the NF variant was 813 on 1 March 1945. The aircraft equipped 14 squadrons between 1940–45.

Typical data: One 1,080-hp Rolls-Royce Merlin 8 to give a maximum speed of 256 mph (223 knots) and a maximum range of 830 miles (1,328 km). Initial climb 1,100 ft/min (341 m/min), ceiling 22,400 ft (6,830 m). Loaded weight 9,800 lb (4,455 kg). Span 46 ft 4½ in (14 m), length 40 ft 3 in (12.3 m), height 14 ft (4.3 m). Eight Browning guns in wings; could be armed with two 250-lb (114 kg) bombs beneath wings.

The Vought-Sikorsky Kingfisher was designed as an observation scout for the USN and was the second Vought-Sikorsky type to enter service with the FAA – the other being the Chesapeake dive-bomber. It first entered service with 703 Squadron and others saw service as catapult-launched reconnaissance aircraft with armed merchant cruisers, with the cruisers HMS *Emerald* and *Enterprise*, and were used in the West Indies for trainers.

Powered by a 450-hp Pratt & Whitney Wasp, it had a maximum speed of 171 mph (274 km/h); climb 960 ft/min (293 m/min); range 900 miles (1,440 km) and a service ceiling of 18,200 ft (5,549 m). Span 35 ft 11 in (11 m), length 33 ft 7 in (10 m), height 14 ft 8 in (4.5 m). Loaded weight was 4,980 lb (2,264 kg) and it was armed with 0.30 machineguns, one fixed and one free-mounted; 240-lb (109 kg) bombs below wings.

After the **Sea Hurricane** had proved that a high performance land fighter could operate successfully from a carrier, the FAA decided in 1941 to adapt the Spitfire and a standard VB fitted with an arrester hook was used for the original trials in HMS *Illustrious*. Commander H. P. Bramwell, DSO, DSC, flew that aircraft which also completed catapult trials.

Some 50 VBs were converted to **Seafire 1Bs** with fixed wings, armed with the 'B' wing containing two 20-mm cannons and four machineguns. The Mk IIC was the next variant with a strengthened airframe for catapult gear and a 'C' wing with four 20-mm cannons.

The Seafire 3 was the first with a manually folded wing enabling the hangar lifts to be used and facilitating deck handling. Variants were the FR3 fitted with two F24 cameras and the LF3, low altitude fighter.

Seafires first went to 807 Squadron in June 1942 and 801 Squadron
in the September, when they embarked in the *Furious* and took part in
the Allied invasion of North Africa. First victim was Dewoitine D520
fighter shot down by Sub-Lieutenant G. C. Baldwin, DSC, on 8
November 1942. By 1943, Seafires equipped 8 squadrons in strike
carriers and 4 squadrons in escort carriers received six each. Shown
above is a striking photograph of a post-war Seafire and below, a deck-
handling party secures Seafires in HMS *Eagle*.

The North African and Salerno landings were covered by Seafire Squadrons from the *Formidable*, *Illustrious*, and escort carriers *Attacker*, *Battler*, *Hunter* and *Stalker* as land-based fighters were out of range. In the Far East when the FAA concentrated a massive strike force against the Japanese, the Seafire 3 was operated by eight squadrons, this time in the *Indefatigable*, *Indomitable*, and the escort carriers *Hunter*, *Stalker*, *Attacker* and *Chaser*. On VJ-Day 12 front-line squadrons were equipped with Seafires. They were phased out of front-line service after the war, but remained with No. 1 Naval Air Fighter School's 759 Squadron, RNAS Yeovilton, until 1946.

Typical performance figures were: maximum speed 365 mph (584 km/h) at 16,000 ft (4,878 m); climb to 20,000 ft (6,098 m) in 7½ min; range 770 miles with drop tank. Span 36 ft 8 in (11 m); length 30 ft (9 m); height 11 ft 2 in (3.4 m). Loaded weight 7,200 lb (3,272 kg). Service ceiling 35,400 ft (11,098 m).

At one period of the war it seemed that the production of modern types of aircraft for the Fleet Air Arm was very slow, and certainly the **Barracuda Mks 1–3** were a long time in reaching operational squadrons. It made its operational debut in the attack on the *Tirpitz* on 3 April 1944; up until then, most similar attacks had been made by Swordfish or Skuas.

The trouble with the Barracuda, as with many other types of early naval aircraft, was that they were intended for multiple roles. It was cluttered up with radomes, radar, lifeboats, mines, torpedoes, and could even be used for dropping agents in France. It still proved a valuable addition to naval strike power during the latter years of the war. The prototype first flew on 7 December 1940 and was the FAA's first all-metal monoplane torpedo bomber.

The prototype made its first deck-landing trials on 18 May 1941 and, from the Mk2 onwards, a 1,640-hp Merlin was fitted with a four-blade propeller instead of the earlier three-bladed one. The Mk3 was for A/S duties and mounted a ASV Mk10 scanner in a radome below the rear of the fuselage.

The Mk2 entered service on 10 January 1943 with 827 Squadron, Stretton, Cheshire, and the force increased during 1943–1944, equipping 12 squadrons.

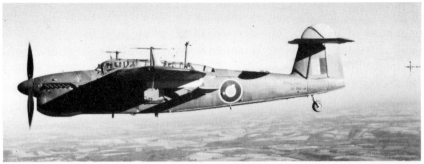

The famous assault on the *Tirpitz* took place when the battleship was berthed in Kaafiord, North Norway, and was attacked by a strike force of Barracudas from *Furious, Victorious, Emperor, Fencer, Pursuer,* and *Searcher.* The *Tirpitz* received 15 direct hits and several near misses from the 1,000-lb and 500-lb bombs. Those taking part came from 827, 829, 830 Squadrons (*Victorious*), 831 (*Furious*), with cover from 800 Squadron (Hellcats), 801 (Seafires), 898 (Wildcats) and 1834 (Corsairs).

At the beginning of 1946, only three operational squadrons remained. One squadron was reformed in 1947 when 815 Squadron took over 12 Barracuda 3s from 744 Training Squadron, and operated them until superseded by the Grumman Avenger in 1953.

Typical data: one 1,260-hp or 1,640-hp Rolls-Royce Merlin, maximum speed 235 mph (205 knots); range 524 miles (838 km) with 2,000-lb of bombs (909 kg) or 686 miles (1,098 km) with a 1,620-lb (736 kg) torpedo. Climb 4½ min to 5,000 ft (1,525 m). Span 49 ft 2 in (15 m); length 39 ft 9 in (12 m); height 15 ft 1 in (4.6 m). Service ceiling 20,000 ft; all-up weight 14,100 lb (6,409 kg).

The prototype **Grumman Hellcat** flew on 26 June 1942. In 1943 they were made available to the RN under the Lease-Lend Agreement, a total of 1,182 being delivered. The first squadron to equip was 800 on 1 July 1943, replacing the Sea Hurricanes. They virtually made up the fighter cover for the British Pacific Fleet with 800 Squadron in the *Emperor*, 808 (*Khedive*), 888 (*Empress*), 1840 (*Indefatigable*), 1844 (*Indomitable*).

By the end of the war there were 14 operational squadrons of Hellcats. By 1946 there were only 2. Typical data: One 2,000-hp Pratt & Whitney Double Wasp giving a maximum speed of 331 mph at sea level (288 knots) and a service ceiling of 36,700 ft (11,190 m). Span 42 ft 10 in (13 m), 16 ft 2 in wings folded (5 m); length 33 ft 7 in (10.2 m); height 14 ft 5 in (4.4 m). All-up weight 13,753 lb (6,252 kg); initial climb 3,410 ft/min (1,040 m). Armed with six 0.5 in machine-guns in wings and provision for six 60-lb (27 kg) rockets or two 1,000-lb (455 kg) bombs beneath wings or centre section. Maximum range at 160 mph (139 knots) was 1,530 miles (2,448 km).

The 600-mile Atlantic Gap when convoys were out of range of aircraft operating from shore bases on both sides of the Atlantic caused a great deal of concern. Focke Wulf Condors from France ranged the Atlantic at will and between August 1940 and February 1941, destroyed over 300,000 ton of shipping. The only real protection was ship-borne aircraft. Carriers, however, were in short supply, despite the most ambitious building programme in FAA history, which saw seven carriers laid down between 1935–1939.

The Director of Air Materiel suggested fitting a simple flight-deck, catapult and arrester wires to suitable merchant ships. As a first step they would continue their normal function of cargo carrying. These Merchant Ship Carriers – MAC ships – were to carry up to six fighters but would have no hangar. Hawkers were asked in October 1940 if Hurricane Mk1s could be modified for catapult work, and such was the urgency that a prototype was ready in five weeks. It was then decided to order catapult equipment for 50 merchant ships – CAM ships, Catapult Assisted Merchant Ships using Fulmar two-seat fighters.

About 50 Hurricane conversions were made and the Admiralty selected the Ocean Boarding Vessels *Ariguani*, *Patia*, *Maplin*, *Springbank*, and the old seaplane carrier *Pegasus* (former *Ark Royal*), to be converted with catapult and fighters. By April 1941 four CAM ships were ready for sea and the first pilot to be catapulted successfully was Sub-Lieutenant M. A. Birrell, from the *Michael E* on 27 May.

The first Merchant Ship Fighter Unit trial launch from the *Empire Rainbow* on 31 May failed, but the second on 4 June succeeded. Other conversions followed including the *Empire Sun*, *Ocean City* and *Novelist*. An 8,000-ton captured German merchantman, the *Hanover*, was also completed with a flight-deck 420 ft (128 m) long, six Grumman Wildcats, a wire crash barrier and two arrester wires.

The first success was on 3 August 1941 when the *Maplin* launched Lieutenant R. W. H. Everett, RNVR, and he shot down a Condor. He ditched and was picked up by the destroyer HMS *Wanderer*.

By June 1942, over 30 escort carriers were on order but they were unlikely to be available until the autumn and most were already committed to the North African landings as they became available.

Grain ships and six tankers were also approved for conversion, and the first of these was the *Rapana*, which entered service in July 1943 with a flight-deck 460 ft (140 m) by 62 ft (19 m), hydraulic arrester wires and a crash barrier. They played a significant role in keeping the sea-lanes open, and by the end of the war they had carried out 170 round trips across the Atlantic, spent 1,183 days flying and lost 114 aircraft.

The Chance Vought Corsair ranks with the Seafire and Sea Hurricane as one of the great fighters of the era. When it first flew in 1940, it was the most powerful naval fighter in the world, with a Pratt & Whitney 1,850-hp engine. This was later improved to one of 2,100 hp. It had the folding inverted gull wing for easier stowage in carriers, and a new technique of spot welding the skin covering reduced drag to a minimum.

The Corsair Mk1 as shown here first equipped 1830 Squadron at the US Naval Base, Quonset, on 1 June 1943. During the year seven other squadrons formed, 1831, 1833 (1 July); 1834 (15 July); 1835, 1836 (15 August); 1837 (1 September); and 1838 (10 October).

In 1944 they equipped 1841 (1 March), 1842 (1 April), 1843 (1 May), 1845 (1 June), 1846, 1848 (1 July), 1849, 1850 (1 August), and 1851 (1 September). During 1945 they equipped 1852 (1 February), and 1853 (1 April) – completing a total of 19 squadrons.

They first saw action when 1834 Squadron (*Victorious*) joined Hellcats, Wildcats and Seafires, in giving fighter cover for the attack on the *Tirpitz*, 3 April 1944. Corsair Mk2s were modified with clipped wings for easier stowage in British carriers and provision for carrying up to 2,000 lb of bombs (909 kg).

The aircraft had a span of 41 ft (12.5 m), the Mk2 only 39 ft 8 in (12 m); length was 33 ft 3 in (10 m), height 15 ft 1 in (4.6 m), and initial climb 1,852 ft/min (565 m/min). Armed with four fixed 0.50 machine-guns in the wings, it had a service ceiling of 34,500 ft (10,518 m) and a maximum speed of 374 mph (325 knots). Range was 675 miles (1,080 km) and loaded weight 11,800 lb (5,364 kg).

The achievements of British naval operations during the war were more than could have been hoped for when it started. *Bismarck*, Matapan, Taranto, Dakar, Oran, had all shown that capital ships were vulnerable to torpedo attacks from the air, but these successes tended to obscure the routine operations which were just as important.

The solid but unspectacular successes of the FAA were in the safe arrivals of merchant ships in convoy, afforded virtual immunity from air or submarine attack by the use of escort carriers and merchant ship conversions, and by the establishment of amphibious beach-heads under the protection of carrier aircraft.

When the elimination of German surface sea power allowed the Navy to deploy its Fleet carriers and support groups to the Pacific, the new techniques developed in that war were quickly mastered and the British Pacific Fleet could fairly claim to have achieved an expertise at least equal to that of the USN, at a speed they had been reluctant to believe possible.

In the early stages of the build-up, the BPF just did not have the afloat support needed on the scale envisaged by the planners, and the variety of ships pressed into Fleet Train service were, on the whole, operationally inefficient and too few in numbers.

Yet the Pacific Ocean became the stage on which the Fleet Air Arm played a leading role, with the greatest concentration of British naval air power in history. Early in 1944, the *Hermes* was in the Indian Ocean, the *Indomitable* had run aground during trials in the West Indies, and the *Victorious* and *Formidable* were unavailable.

Hermes was too old and too small. The *Illustrious* had only Barracudas and Fulmars and these were no match for the Japanese Zeros armed with machine-guns and cannons. To make up deficiencies, the repair ship *Unicorn* was used as a light fleet carrier, together with the escort carriers *Shah* and *Begum*. It was with this small force that Admiral Somerville launched the first air strikes of 46 bombers and 40 fighters against the Japanese base of Sabang, Sumatra. They destroyed 24 aircraft on the ground, hit oil installations and sank two merchant ships. This brilliantly executed raid demonstrated yet again the value of even limited air power at sea.

In November, Admiral Sir Philip Vian arrived to take command of the Aircraft Carrier Squadron, and in December we had the *Indomitable* (Flag), *Illustrious*, *Victorious*, and *Indefatigable*. On 16 January 1945, the Fleet sailed from Trincomalee for the last time, to launch the most devastating attacks so far against the oil refineries at Songei Gerong, Pladjoe and Palembang.

Among the American ideas adopted was the appointment of an

experienced officer as Air Co-ordinator, whose job was to overfly and select targets, and then fly with the raid to re-adjust planned support or divert to other targets. The first officers selected were Major R. C. Hay, RM, (later Lt-Col.) and Commander N. S. Luard.

Because of their short range, *Indefatigable* used her Seafires for air cover, with *Illustrious* and *Victorious* providing 12 Corsairs each, to shoot up enemy airfields before the main strike went in. The strike on 24 January had Avengers armed with 500-lb bombs, and Fireflies with rockets. At Lembak 34 aircraft were destroyed on the ground, and in fierce air combats we claimed 13 down with 6 probables, for the loss of 6 Corsairs and a Hellcat.

On 29 January, after refuelling, a second attack was launched with 48 Avengers, 24 Corsairs, 16 Hellcats and 10 Fireflies. This tremendous morale-boosting attack accounted for 38 aircraft on the ground, with 30 shot down in combat and 7 probables, for the loss of 6 shot down and 25 damaged or lost through deck-landing or ditching.

On 4 February the Fleet was in Fremantle, Australia, preparing for Operation Iceberg. The Fleet carriers embarked 207 aircraft, with support provided by *Striker* (spare aircraft) and despite hits by suicide planes on *Indefatigable*, *Victorious* and *Formidable*, they softened up the airfield ready for the Okinawa assault on 1 April. On 24 July, Lieutenant-Commander A. J. Griffin, RNVR, led an attack on the carrier *Kaiyo* which left her on fire and sinking, with a broken back.

On VJ-Day, the BPF disposition was: **Fleet Carriers,** *Victorious* (Rear-Admiral M. M. Denny), *Formidable* (Captain W. G. Andrews), *Indefatigable* (Captain Graham), *Indomitable* (Captain J. A. S. Eccles), *Colossus* (Captain G. H. Strokes), *Glory* (Captain A. W. Buzzard), *Venerable* (Captain W. A. Dallmeyer), *Illustrious* (Captain W. D. Stephens), and *Implacable* (Captain C. C. Hughes-Hallet).

Escort Carriers: *Striker* (replenishment, Captain W. P. Carne), *Arbiter* (Captain D. H. Everett), *Chaser* (Captain R. G. Poole), *Ruler* (Captain H. P. Currey), *Slinger* (Lieutenant-Commander J. G. Hopkins), *Speaker* (Captain U. H. Jones), *Vindex* (ferry, Commander J. D. Williams), *Fencer* (Lieutenant-Commander A. M. Harris and *Reaper* (Commander T. Clark).

Air Maintenance Ships: *Pioneer, Unicorn, Deer Sound.*

Squadrons: Seafires, 801, 802, 809, 880, 885, 894, 897, 899. Avengers, 820, 828, 832, 848, 849, 854, 857. Corsairs, 1830, 1831, 1833, 1834, 1836, 1837, 1841, 1842, 1845, 1846, 1850, 1851. Fireflies, 1770, 1771, 1772. Hellcats, 888, 892, 1839, 1840, 1844.

Some 1,000 Grumman Avengers served with the FAA during the Second World War and formed 15 FAA Squadrons operating from escort carriers, strike carriers and from shore bases. It was the first American-designed aircraft with a power-operated turret and the first with a 22-inch torpedo. The FAA aircraft were delivered under the Lease-Lend Agreement and were known first as Tarpons and later as Avengers. On 1 January 1943, 832 Squadron (Albacores) took delivery of the first aircraft in Norfolk, Virginia, and operated from the USS *Saratoga* during the landings in the Solomon Islands and the Coral Sea – the first time FAA aircraft operated from an American carrier on active service.

Early in 1953 it was officially announced that the Avenger (above) was again to enter FAA service to strengthen A/S forces, pending the arrival in service of the Fairey Gannet. Pictured here is an Avenger AS4 (XB396) which equipped 824 Squadron and, in 1954, 820 Squadron.

The Reliant, built by the Stinson Division of Vultee Aircraft Inc. (Michigan) taught naval pilots aerial navigation.

The Sea Otter joined the FAA in 1944, superseding the Walrus for ASR and communication duties. The last biplane amphibian designed by Supermarine, it had a tractor lay-out, higher speed, and greater range than the Walrus. The Otter joined 1700 Squadron, Lee-on-Solent, in November 1944, and their six aircraft later embarked in HMS *Khedive*.

Powered by a Bristol Mercury 30 of 855-hp, it had a span of 46 ft (14 m), a length of 39 ft 5 in (12 m), a height of 16 ft 2 in (5 m), and an all-up weight of 10,000 lb (4,546 kg). Maximum speed was 150 mph (130 knots). Range was 565 miles (904 km), service ceiling 16,000 ft (4,878 m), and it was armed with two Vickers K guns amidships and one in the bows.

The de Havilland Sea Mosquito introduced twin-engined aircraft to the FAA but only six were delivered, fitted with British radar and a scanner in the nose. They were fitted with two Rolls-Royce Merlins and had a maximum speed of 345 mph (298 knots) at sea level.

The Sea Hornet F20 pictured below was the first twin-engined single-seat fighter to operate from FAA carriers. Early production aircraft did trials with 703 Squadron, Lee-on-Solent. The first front-line squadron was 801 formed at Ford 1 June 1947. The squadron embarked in *Implacable* during 1949 and flew Hornets until 1951 when they equipped with Sea Furies. The aircraft continued in second-line units until 1955.

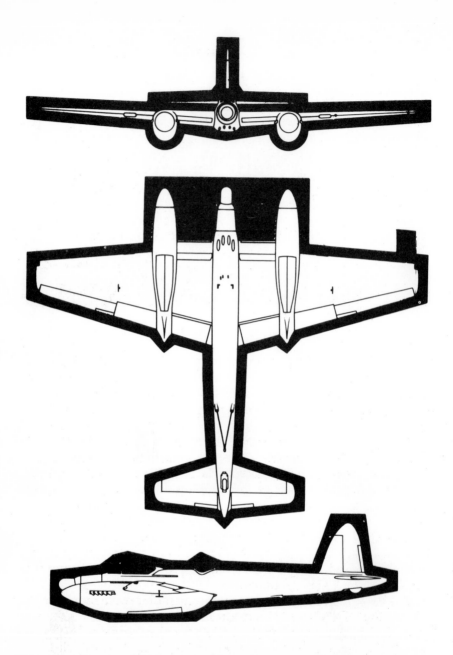

An outline drawing of the de Havilland-built NF21 whose precision radar gave them a useful role in 'pathfinding' on strike attacks. After being replaced they served as radar trainers for second-line squadrons.

122

The NF21 was the only two-seat version of the Hornet and from 1949–1954 was the FAA's standard night fighter. It had an ASH scanner in the nose, folding wings and a long dorsal fin fillet. It entered service with 809 Squadron formed especially for the night fighter role at RNAS Culdrose, on 20 January 1949. It was the only front-line squadron to fly the type, until re-equipped with Sea Venoms in 1954. In November 1951, one aircraft demonstrated its ability flying non-stop from Gibraltar to Lee-on-Solent, averaging 378 mph (329 knots).

After 1954, NF21s served on radar training duties with second-line squadrons and one aircraft was with the FRU at Hurn until late 1955.

Typical data: powered by two Rolls-Royce Merlin engines of 2,030-hp, it had a maximum speed of 365 mph (318 knots) at sea level, a service ceiling of 36,500 ft (11,128 m), and a range of 1,500 miles (2,400 km). Its span was 45 ft (13.8 m), length 37 ft (11 m), height 14 ft (4.3 m) and loaded weight 19,530 lb (8,877 kg). It was armed with four 20-mm cannons forward, and could carry eight 60-lb (27 kg) rocket projectiles or two 1,000-lb (455 kg) bombs.

The PR22 featured above was the photographic reconnaissance (PR) variant used by 801 and 738 Squadrons and was fitted with two F52 cameras for day use or a Fairchild K19B for night pictures. Loaded weight (day) was 16,804 lb (7,638 kg) or (night) 18,230 lb (8,286 kg). Maximum speed was given as 467 mph (406 knots) at 22,000 ft (6,707 m), and service ceiling was 37,500 ft (11,433 m). The Hornets were replaced by Sea Venoms.

The Sea Fury F10 was not only the last piston-engined fighter to operate with front-line squadrons, but was the FAA's leading single-seat fighter from 1947–1954. Driven by a huge five-bladed propeller in front of a cowled engine, sculptured fuselage and wings, it was the result of years of expertise in design and the peak of propeller-driven fighter building. It came too late for the Second World War, but when finally tested in the Korean conflict it dealt capably with the faster jet-propelled MiG-15s.

Adapted from Hawker's design for a smaller version of the RAF Tempest, the prototype first flew on 21 February 1945. The aircraft had fixed wings, an arrester hook, and on 3–5 October 1945 it was fitted with a catapult launching strop. After successful catapult trials at RAE Farnborough, the Sea Fury carried out landing and catapult trials in HMS *Illustrious*.

They first entered service with 807 Squadron in August 1947 at Eglinton and, in May 1948, 802 was the first with the FB11. In the Korean War, Furies were operated by 802 (*Ocean*), 807 (*Theseus*), 801, 804 (*Glory*), 805 and 808 (*Sydney*). Used mainly with Fireflies in ground bombing and rocket attacks, an aircraft from 802 flown by Lieutenant P. Carmichael claimed the first MiG-15 to fall to the aircraft.

In November 1951, Sea Furies replaced the Seafire 17s in 1832 RNVR Squadron, and in May the following year 1831 took its aircraft to Malta and became the first RNVR Unit to do annual training overseas.

Bottom left is the T20 two-seat training variant; below, Sea Furies on deck in a severe winter of the Korean War.

Technical data FB11: powered by a Bristol Centaurus 18 of 2,480-hp, it had a maximum speed of 460 mph (400 knots) at 30,000 ft (9,146 m) and reached this height in 10 minutes. Range was 1,040 miles (1,664 km) with two drop tanks. Service ceiling was 35,800 ft (10,915 m), and loaded weight 12,500 lb (5,682 kg).

The FB11 had a wing span of 38 ft 4 in (12 m), 16 ft 1 in (4.9 m) with wings folded. Length was 34 ft 7 in (10.5 m) and height 12 ft 3½ in (3.8 m). It was armed with four 20-mm cannons in the wings and could carry 12 60-lb rocket projectiles or 2 1,000-lb (454.5 kg) bombs below the wings.

The T20 naval variant was a two-seat dual-control trainer with the instructor's cockpit connected to the pupil's cockpit by a perspex canopy. A mirror was tripod-mounted between the cockpits so the instructor could see the reflector gunsight over the head of his pupil during air firing exercises.

The T20 had the same basic dimensions as the FB11, but was slower at maximum speed, 445 mph (387 knots) at 20,000 ft (6,098 m). Initial climb rate was 4,300 ft/min (1,311 m/min), and the loaded weight was 11,930 lb (5,423 kg). From early 1953, Sea Furies were replaced in front-line squadrons by Sea Hawks.

125

One of the surviving Sea Furies being restored at the FAA Museum, RNAS Yeovilton, where it is on display.

With the changeover from piston-engined aircraft to jets, the years 1945–1956 brought far-reaching changes in deck-flying and landing techniques. Very much involved was the **Sea Venom**, developed from the RAF night fighter Venom NF2. The prototype did trials in HMS *Illustrious* on 9 July 1951. The first production FAW20 flew on 27 March 1953; this was followed by the 21 and 22, with two updated engine changes, power-operated ailerons, American radar, clear-view frameless canopy and, later on, Martin-Baker ejection seats.

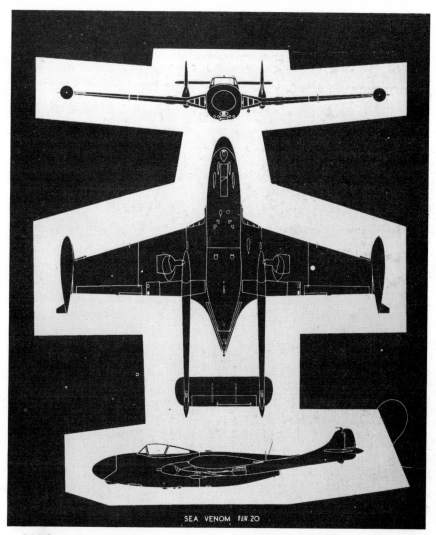

SEA VENOM FAW.20

890 Squadron reformed at Yeovilton on 20 March 1954 with 20s but converted to 21s before carrier operations. The second squadron was 809 which, from 1949, had been the FAA's only all-weather squadron with Sea Hornets.

The *Albion* and *Eagle* operated five squadrons – 809, 891, 893, 894 and 895 – during strikes in accurate ground support operations for the Anglo-French Suez landings. From 1959, the Venom was superseded by the Sea Vixen, but during 1958 three Venoms of 893 (*Victorious*) carried out the first firings of Firestreak guided missiles.

Venoms were the FAA's first jet two-seater all-weather fighter and strike aircraft was powered by a 5,300-lb (2,409 kg) thrust de Havilland Ghost to give a maximum speed of 575 mph (500 knots) with an initial climb of 5,900 ft (1800 m) a minute and a service ceiling of 40,000 ft (12,195 m). Loaded weight was 15,800 lb (7,182 kg); range 705 miles (1,128 km). Armed with four 20-mm guns, eight 60-lb rocket projectiles or bombs below the wings, it had a span of 42 ft 10 in (13 m), a length of 36 ft 8 in (11.2 m), and a height of 8 ft 6 in (2.6 m).

The Sea Balliol T21 was the naval version of the RAF trainer, the prototype of which first flew in October 1952. Thirty were delivered to the FAA, the last on 7 December 1954. It had a Rolls-Royce Merlin 35 of 1,280-hp, and a maximum speed of 288 mph (250 knots).

The Sea Devon, an eight-seat communications aircraft gave valuable service to 781 Squadron, Lee-on-Solent, who received the aircraft in 1955. A total of 13 aircraft were eventually delivered.

These were later supplemented by the de Havilland Sea Heron C20 pictured below, powered by four 250-hp DH Gypsy Queen engines to give a cruising speed of 185 mph (160 knots) at 8,000 ft (2,440 m). Span was 71 ft 6 in (22 m), and the length 48 ft 6 in (14.8 m).

Everyone must have felt in 1946 that the future of British Naval Air Power was assured. Proved in operations throughout the world, the carrier was the modern capital ship and the aircraft the extension of a formidable strike power. An announcement was made that all executive officers were to have preliminary training which would enable them to qualify for a pilot's 'A' licence. The FAA had, after all, including those engaged in support duties, a strength one third of the total in the Royal Navy.

The FAA Command was still unique. The Third Sea Lord was Controller, the Fourth Sea Lord was responsible for Supplies and Transport, and the Civil Lord for Works and Building Ashore. ACNS (Air) was in charge of operations and to co-ordinate their work was the Fifth Sea Lord (Rear-Admiral Sir Thomas Troubridge) who had commanded HMS *Furious* in the early part of the war and then the Air Carrier Group during the invasion of Europe.

The future looked bright as a number of younger captains had commanded carriers during the war. Their influence did not, however, prevent a colossal run down. The escort carriers were handed back to America under the terms of the Lease Lend Agreement and thousands of Avenger, Corsair and Hellcat aircraft were dumped or destroyed. The Royal Navy was left with only Seafires or Fireflies to complement its few remaining operational carriers. In addition to the six Fleet and five Light carriers which had been completed 1940–1945, there were two Fleet carriers building and five programmed, as well as 13 Light Fleet carriers under construction. A year after the end of the war, the RN carrier fleet had dwindled to five Light Fleet carriers with a total of 72 Fireflies and 48 unusable Seafire XVs between them. One Fleet carrier was in commission as a trials and training ship.

On the eve of the Korean War (June 1950) there were four operational carrier groups with 104 Sea Furies, Seafire 47s and Fireflies. The two trial and training carriers had 45 front-line and 41 RNVR aircraft available. After the Korean War, the emphasis was on reduction and concentration, imposed by the ever-increasing cost of aircraft and ships.

The Radical Review of 1954 was followed by the Way Ahead Committee in 1955 and yearly Long Term Defence Costings and Reviews from 1956. Five carriers joined the Fleet between 1951 and 1955 – *Eagle, Ark Royal*, and the improved Light Fleet carriers, *Centaur, Albion* and *Bulwark*. *Victorious* survived the disposal programme and after modernization commissioned as an almost new ship.

The Fairey Firefly was designed as a fast fighter-reconnaissance aircraft (FR), carrying on the tradition of the Hawker Osprey and Fairey Fulmar, the first monoplane of the type which preceded the Firefly.

The F1-NF2 had the more powerful Griffon engine in place of the Merlin and firepower was enhanced by replacing the eight machine-guns with four 20-mm cannons. It proved to be 40 mph faster than the Fulmar and was also fitted with fully retractable Fairey-Youngman flaps which could be extended below and along the trailing edge for improved cruise performance and better manoeuvrability.

The last of a total production of 832 was delivered on 23 November 1946, and in all they equipped 29 squadrons and were firmly established as the FAA's standard FR aircraft. The night fighter variant (NF) had two small radar radomes below the wings and on either side of the fuselage.

The first Mk1 squadron was 1770 RNAS Yeovilton, which formed on 1 October 1943. It later embarked in the *Indefatigable* and first became operational in Norway during the attacks on the *Tirpitz*.

Next was 1771 RNAS Yeovilton, formed on 1 February 1944 (*Indefatigable*). They played a major part in the British Pacific Fleet operations against Japan.

The next variants were the FR4–AS6 range, powered by a two-speed two-stage supercharged Griffon engine and a four-bladed propeller in place of the three-bladed one. There followed the Mk5, the latter being the first with power-folding wings. During the Korean War, Fireflies and Sea Furies played a major role in bombing and rocket strikes against land and sea targets.

In a prolific life spanning 13 years, Fireflies of various marks equipped a total of 63 squadrons at different times. The type later emerged exclusively as anti-submarine aircraft like the AS6 (WD918) pictured above and (WJ 154) below. The first aircraft went to 1830 Squadron, Abbotsinch, in November 1951, and the squadron operated it until it was replaced with the interim Avenger, and then the Gannet in 1955. The trainer version T1-T3 equipped a total of 11 squadrons.

Typical data: Rolls-Royce Griffon 1,965-hp engine giving a speed of 300 mph (260 knots), a service ceiling of 25,500 ft (7,775 m), initial climb 1550 ft/min (47.25 m/min), and a range of 860 miles (1,376 km). Loaded weight was 13,970 lb (6,350 kg), span 44 ft 6 in (13.6 m), length 38 ft 3 in (11.7 m), and height 13 ft 3 in (4 m). No armament. The AS6 could be armed with 16 × 50-lb (27 kg) rockets or two 1,000-lb (454 kg) bombs below the wings.

By 1957, the Fifth Sea Lord was responsible for the fighting efficiency of the FAA including all aspects of operational and tactical policy. Under him were two Staff Divisions concerned with Naval Air Warfare, and Naval Organization and Training. Two other Divisions, also at Admiralty, were concerned with procurement and maintenance of aircraft – air equipment (DAE) and maintenance and repair (DAMR). They were responsible to the Third Sea Lord and Controller. The Ministry of Supply was responsible for supplying aircraft and equipment and an SNO was Deputy Controller of Aircraft at that Ministry.

The broad Admiralty policy was implemented by Flag Officer Air (Home) for Naval Air Stations within the UK, and by Flag Officer Aircraft Carriers as it concerned the Fleet. Flying and ground training were separated under the respective commands of Flag Officer Flying Training; a Staff Captain under Home Air for training; and the Flag Officer Reserve Aircraft.

In January 1957, the training of National Service aircrews ended. Admiral Sir Caspar John, KCB, then Flag Officer Air Home, had just completed 32 years with the FAA and wrote: "I have never known the Fleet Air Arm in better heart and I judge it to be a far more effective weapon system than it has ever been."

Vice-Admiral M. L. Power, CB, CBE, DSO, was Flag Officer Aircraft Carriers, commanding the new spearhead of the Navy, and he said: "Carrier flying remains a specially skilled and inherently hazardous operation, demanding a very high standard of discipline and training . . . in Korea virtually the entire British air effort was carrier borne and was maintained over three years." He went on to postulate that carriers should work in pairs, providing the tactical mobility of the aircraft with the strategic mobility of the ship. Has the role of the carrier ever been better expressed?

Aircraft then in front-line service included Gannet AS1s and AS4s, Sea Hawks, Sea Venoms, Wyverns, Skyraider AEW, with Hiller, Dragonfly and Whirlwind helicopters. Each Naval Air Station and carrier had a resident helicopter flight. The only front-line helicopter squadron was 845, flying Whirlwinds with dipping sonar. FOFT (Yeovilton) was responsible for RNAS Culdrose, Lossiemouth, Eglington, Ford and Brawdy.

The Hawker Sea Hawk superseded the Attacker jet fighter and Sea Furies in the FAA and entered service with 806 Squadron in March 1953, before the squadron embarked in HMS *Eagle*. The F1 was superseded by the F2 with power-boosted ailerons and the FB3 with strengthened wings for external loads. The last production model for the FAA was the FGA6.

This single-seater ground-attack fighter armed with 4 fixed 2-mm guns in the fuselage, and 10 rocket projectiles or 2 500-lb bombs below the wings, was flown by 800, 802, 804, 810, 897 and 899 Squadrons from the *Eagle*, *Albion* and *Bulwark*, during the Anglo-French Suez landings of 1956. The last squadron was 806 which disbanded at Brawdy on 15 December 1960, after returning from the Far East in the *Albion*.

The Sea Hawk was powered by a Rolls-Royce Nene of 5,200-lb thrust to give a maximum speed at sea level of 518 mph (446 knots) and had an initial climb of 5,700 ft (1,738 m) a minute. Service ceiling was 44,500 ft (13,567 m) and loaded weight with two 100-gallon drop tanks was 16,200 lb (7,364 kg). Span was 39 ft (12 m), 13 ft 4 ins (4 m) folded; length was 39 ft 10 ins (12 m), and height 8 ft 9 ins (2.7 m).

Above Sea Hawk jet fighters are being launched by catapult from the *Eagle*. The catapult team in protective clothing crouch at deck level to reduce the wind pressure and cover their ears to shut out the roar. Seen below is a Sea Hawk about to hook a wire as it lands on.

The Douglas Skyraider reached 778 Squadron, RNAS Culdrose in 1951 and after carrier trials in the *Eagle*, became operational with 849 Squadron in 1953. 849 operated a Headquarters Flight permanently based at Culdrose, and four Flights (A, B, C, D) for detached duties with carriers. Supplied under the Mutual Defence Assistance Programme (MDAP), they were the first purpose-built AEW aircraft operated by the RN and carried nearly a ton of sophisticated radar and electronics. This technique was pioneered by the USN during the Second World War with the Grumman Avenger.

The Skyraider AEW1 was one of the last piston-engined fixed-wing aircraft in the FAA and was replaced by the Gannet. Typical data: powered by a 2,700-hp Wright Cyclone, it cruised at 250 mph (218 knots), had a range of 3,000 miles (4,800 km), carried no armament, and the loaded weight was 25,000 lb (11,364 kg). Span was 50 ft (15 m), length 39 ft 3 in (12 m), and height 15 ft 8 in (4.8 m). It was a three-seat radar picket and eventually left operational service in 1960.

The Fairey Gannet was the first FAA aircraft to combine search and strike and, except for rockets, was the first to carry all its weapon load internally. It was the first naval aircraft in the world to fly with a double airscrew engine unit which combined the economy of single-engine operation when needed, and the extra speed for combat operations when the thrust of both propellers was used. Each half of the famed Double Mamba could be controlled separately with one engine shut down and the propeller feathered for long-range cruising.

The Mamba was designed to run on kerosene, naval diesel or turbine fuel and aided the Admiralty policy of doing away with petrol stores in aircraft carriers.

On 19 June 1950 the prototype made the first-ever landing on a British carrier, HMS *Illustrious*, and the first operational squadron 826 formed at Lee-on-Solent 17 January 1955. From that time until the *Ark Royal* was phased out in 1979, it was the mainstay of the carrier A/S forces and of the AEW, long-range airborne early warning system. 826 embarked in the *Eagle* in May 1955. A T Mk2 is featured above.

In 1955, a dual-control trainer T2 made its first appearance; it differed from the AS1 in not having a retractable radome, dual control in the observer's cockpit and an additional periscope. The first production model flew on 1 March 1957.

The Gannet AEW3 was designed as a replacement for the Douglas Skyraider, the standard AEW aircraft in the FAA since 1952. The new fuselage incorporated a large fuselage radome, new fin and rudder, and a more powerful Double Mamba. XJ440 made the first deck-landing trials in HMS *Centaur* on 18 November 1958, and 700G Flight (Lieutenant-Commander W. Halwey) did the Intensive Flying Trials. In July 1960, 849 Squadron 'C' Flight embarked in the *Hermes*.

The power wing-folding sequence (*above*) was another asset. In 1970 the last Fairey aircraft on front-line service went to sea in the *Ark Royal*. These were XL482, 494, XP229 and XR433, of 849 Squadron.

Powered by a Double Mamba 102, of 3,875-ehp, the AEW3 had a maximum speed of 250 mph (218 knots), a range of 700 miles (1,120 km), a service ceiling of 25,000 ft (7,622 m), and a cruising endurance of 5–6 hours. It was not armed. Span was 54 ft 4 in (16.5 m), length 44 ft (13.5 m), and height 16 ft 10 in (5 m).

The Westland Wyvern TF1, torpedo strike fighter, first flew on 12 December 1946 and was used for carrier-handling trials in the *Eagle* during 1952. The TF2 was the first variant with a turbo-prop engine, the 4,030-ehp Rolls-Royce Clyde. It first flew in January 1949.

The first Westland-designed aircraft for the FAA since their Walrus, was to be fitted with a variety of engines and took seven years to reach operational squadrons. It was the first designed for turbo-prop operation, but the engines did not become available until 1948. It flew for the first time in 1951 and entered service with 813 Squadron in May 1953, embarking in the *Eagle* during 1954, and later in the *Albion*. A second squadron, 827, joined the *Eagle* in 1955 and in the November, 830 and 831 reformed with Wyverns at RNAS Ford. 831 was the only squadron to use them in a war role during the Suez operations of November 1956. 813 Squadron was the last to use the aircraft, and was disbanded in March 1958.

Taken in 1957, this Wyvern from 813 Squadron, HMS *Eagle*, is seen flying over the rugged mountainous country of Northern Norway, within the Arctic Circle, during a series of NATO exercises.

Typical data: one 4,110-ehp Armstrong Siddeley Python, 383 mph (333 knots) sea level; ceiling 28,000 ft (8,537 m); range 900 miles, initial climb 2,350 ft/min (716.5 m/min). Span 44 ft (13.5 m), 20 ft folded (6 m); length 42 ft 3 in (13 m); height 15 ft 9 in (4.8 m). Maximum loaded weight 24,500 lb (11,136 kg).

This unusual view could almost be called 'tails up'; it shows a Wyvern from the rear and the distinctive configuration of the wings.

The School of Aircraft Handling was at Lossiemouth; safety equipment ratings were at Seafield Park near Gosport; naval airmen (photographers) at Ford; meteorological training at Kete and air mechanics were trained at Bramcote. Parallel streams of radio and electrical specialists were trained at HMS *Collingwood*, Fareham, and later at HMS *Ariel*, Worthy Down. The WRNS had five specializations open to them: air mechanics (airframes or engines), radio (air), range assessors, air stores and met. observers.

RNAS Arbroath was the Headquarters of FORA who was the Naval Air Equipment Authority (UK), co-ordinating the work of the aircraft repair yards at Fleetlands (near Lee-on-Solent), Donibristle (Scotland), and Belfast.

The FAA was a very important part of the Navy's defence and strike capability and led the world in experiment with pure jets operating from carriers. On 3–4 December 1945, a modified Sea Vampire piloted by Lieutenant-Commander E. M. 'Winkle' Brown, did trials from HMS *Ocean* and was the first pure jet aircraft to operate from a British carrier.

The Royal Navy also led the world in introducing three inventions which enabled the aircraft carrier to deal efficiently with faster jets – the angled flight-deck, the steam catapult and the mirror landing sight.

With the greater speeds and higher wing-loading of modern aircraft, it was becoming increasingly difficult to follow the old system, introduced around 1939, of using the first third of the flight-deck for catapult take-off and parked aircraft, and the after two-thirds for landings, with the two areas separated by a crash barrier of wire rope. The crash or safety barrier was introduced to protect the parked aircraft. They could therefore be safely moved down to the hangar by the lift as other aircraft landed on.

Space on a flight-deck has always been at a premium and it was impossible to increase size without making the carrier much bigger, and it was all too common for landing aircraft missing the arrester wires, to penetrate the barrier and end up among the parked aircraft with disastrous results.

In 1952, Captain D. R. F. C. Campbell, DSC, RN, and Mr L. Boddington of RAE, suggested that the landing area could be separated from the parking area by angling the flight-deck a few degrees off to the port side of the carrier's centre line. An aircraft overshooting then had an unobstructed flight path ahead and could go round again if necessary.

The benefits of this elegantly simple solution were immediate and obvious. Approaches and touch-downs could be practised while the forward area was full of parked aircraft. Used with the mirror landing sight, deck-landing accidents were reduced to about a third of their former rate, and the training effort by a quarter.

The new inventions of the angled deck and the short-stroke steam catapult were to some extent complementary as they allowed landings and take-offs to carry on simultaneously and speeded up flying operations. The first aircraft carrier with an angled deck was HMS *Centaur*.

Catapult trials took place during 1917 from HMS *Slinger*, but the first really successful design which could be powered by compressed air or cordite, was designed by R. F. Carey and mounted in the cruiser HMS *Vindictive* for trials. In October 1925, a Fairey IIID piloted by Wing Commander E. J. P. Burling became the first British aircraft to be catapulted off the *Vindictive* using the Carey catapult.

Two years later, the first air-operated catapult was installed in HMS *Frobisher* and many variations followed in cruisers and battleships. A quite remarkable use of the catapult was in HM Submarine *M2*, built by Vickers at Barrow, which commissioned in November 1919. She was converted in 1920s to a submersible seaplane carrier with the forward 12-inch gun replaced by a hangar with a watertight door. The Parnall Peto was a small two-seater reconnaissance aircraft and was launched from a catapult which ran nearly the entire length of the submarine's forecastle. On 26 January 1932, after a series of useful experiments, M2 was lost with her crew of 60 and was found later off Portland with the hangar door, and the door between hangar and pressure hull, open.

The steam catapult was originally designed by Mr C. C. Mitchell, OBE, a former Naval Commander of Brown Brothers, Edinburgh. Subsequent development was largely vested in the Naval Air Department, RAE Bedford.

In equipments prior to the steam catapult, the power was derived from a hydro-pneumatic unit below deck which transmitted the accelerating force to the aircraft by flexible steel ropes working round pulleys. Increases in aircraft weight and a requirement for high launching speeds, with much larger increases in ropes and pulleys, showed a limit had been reached with this design.

The steam catapult employed a launching shuttle accelerating the aircraft by a launch bridle, propelled by two pistons in two slotted cylinders side by side under the deck, along the whole accelerating stroke. A hydraulic retarding system arrested the piston assembly and shuttle at the end of the launch. The first steam catapult was installed for trials in HMS *Perseus* during 1950 and it was finally demonstrated to the USN in 1951. Developments have been actively pursued by naval Fleet Air Arms throughout the world since.

For many years through to the 1950s, a feature of flying operations was the 'batman' who stood on the edge of the flight deck equipped with a pair of coloured paddles, by means of which he signalled orders to landing aircraft. Despite long training and experience, his expertise was being taxed to the utmost with the ever-increasing approach speeds of modern aircraft.

The Sea Fury introduced in 1947 raised approach speeds to about 90–95 knots and the old style of steep descending approach, followed by flare out and engine cut, was modified in 1948 to nearly level approach at higher speeds. The method became impossible with jet fighters with approach speeds in the 140–150 knot range, and the introduction of the mirror landing sight eliminated the time lag between the batman's signal and pilot reaction, which could be disastrous at such speeds.

In 1952, Commander H. C. N. 'Nick' Goodhart, RN, proposed the investigation of a simple optical device which would give the pilot continuous visual information of his position relative to the flight-deck. By 'zeroing' in on the device, the aircraft could be brought in on a fixed flight path with no 'flare' and no 'cut' until an arrester wire was engaged. The angle and position of the device had to be chosen to give adequate clearance over the round down, touch-down at the required point on deck, and an acceptable rate of descent for undercarriage protection.

Simply put, a large mirror reflected a light system so that the pilot saw a round 'blob'. The mid-point of the mirror was defined for the pilot by a horizontal row of lights on either side of it. On the correct glide path, the pilot saw the reflected light source or 'blob' lined up with two horizontal bars of light. If too high, the light source appeared above the horizontal bars and if too low, the light source moved below the central horizontal line. By tilting the mirror in phase with, but through the half-angle of the pitching deck, the indicated glide path was stabilized. Flight trails of the prototype, developed by RAE, were conducted in HMS *Illustrious* during 1953 and were immediately successful. Deck-landings were easier, more consistent, and from a range of up to one and a half miles by day and twice this distance at night, the pilot could see his position at a glance.

Following this success, the mirror landing aid was fitted in all operational carriers of the US and Royal Navies.

The follow-up to this device was the Deck-Landing Projection Sight in which the light source mirror is replaced with a vertical stack of optical projectors. Development was by the Ministry of Supply and the General Electric Company, and in mid-1959 during the *Ark Royal*'s refit, the new landing aid was fitted. Development work was handed over to the Admiralty Director of Electrical Engineering, and further improvements were made, varying from a continuous dimming control to easier access for maintenance and a coarse aid to allow pilots to pick up the sight at long range.

The Short Seamew A/S aircraft was designed for cheap and rapid production and did carrier trials during 1955–1956, when it entered full production. A single-engine monoplane with powered wing-folding and a non-retractable undercarriage, it was powered by a Mamba AS Ma6 engine to give a maximum level speed of 245 mph (211 knots) and a dive speed of 375 mph (325 knots). Maximum weapon load was 2,000 lb (910 kg), and endurance up to 5 hours.

All-up weight was 14,000 lb (6,350 kg) and initial rate of climb 1,600 ft/min (488 m/min), taking nine minutes to reach 10,000 ft (3,050 m). Service ceiling was 24,500 ft (7,470 m); span 55 ft (16.8 m); length 41 ft (12.5 m) and wings folded span 23 ft (7 m).

The FAA's first operational jet fighter squadron was 800 Squadron which received Attackers in August 1951, and by 1955 the transition to jets in first-line squadrons had been completed. Piston-engined aircraft remained in second-line squadrons and for certain specialized duties such as AEW. **The Attacker** has a unique place in FAA history as its first jet fighter and although replaced by Sea Hawks and Sea Venoms only a few years later, is worthy of note. It was the first aircraft to use the Rolls-Royce Nene 3 with 5,100-lb thrust, to give a maximum speed of 590 mph (513 knots) at sea level.

Carrier trials were in the *Illustrious* during 1947 and the first production aircraft flew on 3 April 1950, and the last of 145 aircraft was delivered in 1953. The F1 was superseded by the FB2 and they first entered service with 800 Squadron, Ford, on 22 August 1951.

A single-seat fighter built by the Supermarine Division of Vickers-Armstrong Ltd, it had a span of 36 ft 11 ins (11 m), was 37 ft 6 ins long (11.5 m), and 9 ft 11 ins high (3 m). It weighed 11,500 lb (5,227 kg) loaded, had a range of 590 miles without auxiliary tanks, a service ceiling of 45,000 ft (13,720 m), and was armed with four 20-mm guns in the wings. FB1 was also able to carry 8 60-lb rocket projectiles or 2 1,000-lb bombs below the wings.

The **Scimitar** was the first FAA aircraft capable of carrying an atomic bomb and the first swept-wing transonic aircraft to enter service with 803 Squadron, Lossiemouth, in June 1958. It was a significant advance on the Sea Hawk which it superseded, with blown flaps as a standard fit. It also incorporated for the first time in a British naval aircraft, the Fairey designed power-operated control system.

Four Scimitars of 807 Squadron in 'box' formation during a looping manoeuvre (*Flight photograph*).

The last Scimitar squadron to form, 804, embarked in the *Hermes* in July 1960. This single-seat aircraft was powered by two Rolls-Royce Avon 202 jets to give a maximum 22,500-lb thrust, and a maximum speed of 710 mph (614 knots). Rate of climb was 12,000 ft/min (3,659 m/min), and it was armed with either 40 Aden 30-mm cannons, 4 Sidewinder missiles, or 12 2-in rockets. Loaded weight was 40,000 lb (18,182 kg). It had a span of 37 ft 2 in (11.5 m), a length of 55 ft 4 in (17 m), and a height of 15 ft 3 in (4.7 m).

This photograph shows the 'plan' view of a Scimitar armed with 24 3-inch rocket projectiles (*Flight photograph*).

Entering service shortly after the Scimitar was the two-seater **Sea Vixen,** the FAA's first all-weather swept-wing transonic fighter. It superseded the subsonic Sea Venom.

Service trials with 700Y Flight took place in November 1958 in the carriers *Victorious* and *Centaur*, and the first operational squadron was 892, RNAS Yeovilton, which commissioned 2 July 1959 (Commander M. H. J. Petrie). The following March, the squadron embarked in HMS *Ark Royal*. A second squadron was 890, RNAS Yeovilton, 1 February 1960 which embarked in the new carrier *Hermes* in the July.

The arrival of the Sea Vixen was a big step forward for the FAA, and its ability to protect the Fleet was further enhanced by the introduction of specialized Air Direction Frigates surrounding the carrier task force. It was twice as fast as the Venom and was also the Navy's first aircraft designed as an integrated weapon system with missiles instead of guns. It was armed with Firestreak missiles, a Ferranti pilot attack sight and climbed to 40,000 ft (12,195 m) in 8 minutes. Powered by twin Rolls-Royce Avon jets, each of 11,230-lb thrust, the FAW1 below had a maximum speed of 645 mph (1,032 km/h) at 10,000 ft (3,049 m), and had a service ceiling of 48,000 ft (14,634 m). It had a span of 51 ft (15.5 m), a length of 55 ft 7 in (17 m), and a height of 10 ft 9 in (3.3 m). Armed with 4 Firestreak infra-red homing missiles or 4 rocket packs of 28 × 2-in missiles stowed internally, it could carry 2 1,000-lb (454.5 kg) bombs. All-up weight was 35,000 lb (15,910 kg). From 1964, it was superseded by the FAW2.

Above, the second production FAW1. Below, a Supermarine Scimitar from 803 Squadron is seen about to refuel from a Sea Vixen of 892 Squadron. The aircraft formed part of the *Victorious*'s Air Group. The flight refuelling pods carried on the under-wing pylon of the Vixen allowed any of the carrier's jets to refuel in the air.

One of the last batch of FAW1s refuels a Phantom.

The FAW2 had additional fuel tanks in the tail boom extensions giving greater range and was fitted with a launcher for the new Red Top air-to-air guided missiles. In December 1964, 899 Squadron's aircraft embarked in the *Eagle* and the next year took part in the blockade of Rhodesia.

In October 1968 892 Squadron disbanded and was re-equipped with Phantoms, with 893 disbanding in July 1970 and 766 in December 1970. The last squadron was 899 in the *Eagle* until that carrier was phased out.

A sight not often seen – formation flying by (from the top) Gannets, Sea Vixen, Scimitar, Hunter and Hunter Trainer.

The Hunter GA11 was used for ground attack training by 738 Squadron and this picture was taken at Lossiemouth. It was also used to train students as they progressed from Vampires and Hunter T8s, when front-line squadrons were being equipped with swept-wing fighters like the Scimitar and Sea Vixen. They became well known to visitors at the SBAC Show, Farnborough, when four GA11s formed the Blue Herons aerobatic team in 1975, and at Greenham Common in 1976 and 1977. These aircraft were also used to train Fighter Controllers at RNAS Yeovilton. Powered by a Rolls-Royce Avon turbo-jet of 7,500-lb (3,409 kg) static thrust, they reached Mach 0.94 and had a service ceiling of 50,000 ft (15,244 m). Span 33 ft 8 in (10 m), length 45 ft 10 in (14 m), and loaded weight 17,100 lb (7,773 kg).

Typical operational environment for a Buccaneer on low-level reconnaissance over Norway.

Below, an unusual picture of the dive brakes open, with a mechanic making adjustments in a pre-flight check.

The Buccaneer S2, powered by two Rolls-Royce Spey jet engines, followed the Gyron-engined Mk1, the world's first low-level, high speed aircraft, with a 30% increase in thrust, lower fuel consumption and greater range. Ordered by the RN in 1962, the production model first flew on 6 June 1964. It remained in production until 1968.

The first production model showed its paces on 4 October 1965, when it made the first non-stop crossing of the Atlantic from Goose Bay, Labrador, to RNAS Lossiemouth and covered the 1,950 miles in 4 hrs 16 mins without in-flight refuelling. 801 Squadron formed on 14 October 1965 and the following year embarked in HMS *Victorious*. The aircraft continued in service with the *Eagle* and then the *Ark Royal*.

Designed to find the 'hole' in enemy radar defences, the Buccaneer was a two-seater low-level strike aircraft and its two engines developed 22,000-lb thrust to give a maximum speed of Mach 0.85 at 200 ft (61 m). The wing span was 44 ft (13.5 m), length 63 ft 5 in (19.4 m), and height 16 ft 3 in (4.4 m). It could carry a varied weapon load of 16,000 lb (7,273 kg), and had a range of 3,457 miles (4,800 km).

The S1 (NA39) was the world's first custom-designed low-level strike aircraft designed by Mr B. P. Laight to a Naval Staff Requirement. It was capable of delivering a nuclear weapon and exploiting the gap below radar defences at speeds in excess of Mach 0.9. Manufactured by the Blackburn Aircraft Company, the first operational squadron was 801, who embarked in the *Eagle* on 20 February 1963. Maximum speed was given as 720 mph at sea level, with a weapon load of 8,000 lb (3,636 kg). It had a span of 44 ft (13.5 m), 20 ft folded (6 m), and a tactical radius of 550 miles.

One of the last of the *Ark Royal*'s Buccaneers ready for a 'no hands' take-off.

This unusual view of the Phantom gives an idea of the exceptionally clean aerodynamic lines. The naval variant has a folding nose radome for easier handling in lifts, larger flaps and has a superior performance to the American version from which it was developed, by virtue of its Spey engines.

The McDonnell Douglas Phantom was the first truly supersonic aircraft the FAA operated and the Omega insignia on the tail suggests it might be the last. The first production aircraft (XT858–60) arrived at Yeovilton 29 April 1968, and 700P Trials Unit commissioned next day. On 14 January 1969, 767 Training Squadron commissioned followed by the first operational squadron 801 (Lt-Cdr Brian Davies) 31 March 1969. On 11 May 1969, the CO with Lt-Cdr Peter Goddard (Senior Observer) set a world air-speed record, New York–London, of 4 hours 46 minutes 57 seconds, refuelling from Victor tankers of No. 55 Squadron RAF. The ratified Diploma was presented at RNAS Yeovilton on 10 December. True air speed averaged 1,100 mph (956.5 knots).

Powered by two Rolls-Royce Speys developing 20,515-lb (9,325 kg) thrust in reheat conditions, the Phantom has a top speed of 1,386 mph (1,205 knots); all-up weight 56,000 lb (25,455 kg); initial climb 32,000 ft/min (9,756 m/min), and combat radius 500 miles (800 km). The aircraft is 57 ft 7 in (17.5 m) long; 38 ft 5 in (12.0 m) span and 16 ft 1 in (5.0 m) high. It can be armed with four fuselage-mounted Sparrow and four Sidewinder air-to-air missiles below wings, or up to 10,000 lb (4,546 kg) of conventional bombs, rockets or other missiles, for strike operations.

007 Flies Navy – one of the last Phantoms to fly off the *Ark Royal*.

HELICOPTERS

Either by accident or design, aerial combat between helicopters armed
with missiles and guns will be as commonplace in any future war as
were the early 'dog-fights' over the trenches in mid-1915.

Hare

Hoplite

Hip

Hind

There are only two reasons
for arming helicopters –
offence or defence. Defence is
necessary to survive in a hostile
environment, and an offensive
capability is needed to counter
the threat of missile-armed
Fast Patrol Boats, submarines,
or to support ground
operations. In the early days of
helicopter development,
offensive operations usually
resulted in the single-weapon
solution – the Wasp/AS12
combination for FPB
operations or the Wessex
armed with the Mk44 torpedo
to counter submarines.

These early solutions were
largely negated by the ever-
increasing strength of the
USSR and her Warsaw Pact
allies, which demanded
multiple solutions to a wide
variety of operational
problems. Such is the speed
with which the Russians have
developed helicopter
operations after a late start –
their first Helicopter Bureau
was not formed until 12
December 1947 under the late
M. I. Mil – that the armed
helicopter could now
fundamentally change ground
and air warfare.

The super powers have studied in depth the possibility of air-to-air combat, probably arising from armed helicopters and gunships acting as escorts to attacking ground forces and exploiting the mobility of air power. The natural counter is another well-armed helicopter attack force capable of all-weather operations, with the ability to destroy the enemy helicopters.

We already have the well-proven Westland Lynx capable of looping the loop in the hands of an experienced pilot, and other machines armed with largely forward-firing missiles and automatic weapons. The Helicopter Fighter is surely a weapon of the future.

No one who saw it will forget the spine-tingling displays put on by the Westland Wessex helicopters of 845 Squadron at the 1968 Farnborough Air Show or at a subsequent Aldershot Army Show. Both displays were superb examples of Royal Navy expertise in helicopter operations, built on a firm foundation of vast experience in Commando assaults, close-range attacks by heavily armed gunships and precision flying to the highest standards. You have to be precise to land a 'chopper' on the small flight-deck of a frigate pitching and rolling in a heavy sea, when the rotor clearance between the hangar face and the

The Lynx helicopter XX910 pictured during flying demonstrations at HMS *Daedalus*, Lee-on-Solent, 8 October 1974.

mortars aft is so small. To watch the helicopter approach from astern on the port side and go into a hover, then move slowly sideways about eight feet off the deck until it is positioned with its wheels just above the landing circle, and then land exactly within that area at the direction of the 'batsman', is to watch helicopter flying at its most precise. Naval helicopters have taken part in major and minor operations all over the world, from the heat of the desert and humidity of the jungle, to the snow and ice of the Arctic.

This photograph, taken by the author during a 'Meet the Navy' cruise in HMS *Phoebe*, shows the delicate control needed to land safely on the small flight-deck.

Although the name of Westland Helicopters Limited is synonymous with helicopter flying in the RN, it should not be forgotten that the company had its origins in the engineering firm of Petters Limited who were one of the first companies to respond to Lloyd George's appeal in 1915 for increased effort to produce more munitions. Within 24 hours, company representatives had been invited to a conference at the Admiralty where naval representatives stated their primary need for seaplanes. Petters accepted an initial contract for 12 Short 184s, with a standard Sunbeam engine of 225 hp and a top speed of 75 mph. These were built in a factory constructed on what had been Westland Farm. This was the first torpedo-carrying aircraft to enter service with a naval force anywhere in the world. On 31 May 1916 at the Battle of Jutland, the fourth of the batch (N8359) was the first aircraft to take part in any major sea battle. It was launched from HMS *Engadine* and wirelessed back enemy sighting reports.

Juan de la Cierva's tilting hub and rotor method of control as fitted in the C30 autogiro, provided an aircraft with good response and its military potential was quickly recognized. The first recorded landing of a British autogiro at sea was by a C30 fitted with a 3-blade direct control rotor 37 ft in diameter, powered by a 140-hp Armstrong-Siddeley Genet engine. A landing was made in 1935 by Mr R. A. C. Brie, then Chief Test Pilot for the Cierva Autogiro Company, on the Italian cruiser *Fiume*, anchored off La Spezia. This was followed by several landings and take-offs in the open sea, at speeds of up to 24 knots.

Two C30s were ordered by Admiralty and successful trials took place in the carrier HMS *Furious*. The Navy then ordered five C40s, a side-by-side two-seater, powered by a 180-hp Salmson engine. Two were delivered to the RN before the outbreak of war.

In the UK, the Glasgow engineering firm of G. & J. Weir made a great contribution to autogiro progress, but in 1937 they abandoned these for helicopters. The first was the W5 with a side-by-side rotor configuration, powered by a 50-hp Weir engine. The design embodied fore and aft cyclic control for pitch, differential fore and aft cyclic for yaw, and differential collective for lateral control.

The Sikorsky VS300 was successfully demonstrated in 1939 and Captain Caspar John (later Admiral of the Fleet Sir), Director of Naval Development and Production, sent Wing Commander Brie to America, to interest the Americans in the use of autogiros for A/S duties. Brie worked closely in Washington with another famous naval personality, Lieutenant-Commander Richard Smeeton (later Admiral Sir Richard and Chairman of SBAC).

Brie designed a small platform 90 ft × 40 ft which was fitted to the British merchant ship *Empire Mersey* and in 1942, to demonstrate the value of rotating wing aircraft for small ship use, successful landings were made on HMS *Ranger* and the *Empire Mersey*. The aircraft used was a Pitcairn PA39, a C40 built under licence.

Early in 1942 the prototype Sikorsky XR-4 had been flown and plans put in hand for production. The emphasis placed on the use of helicopters for A/S convoy work by the British Air Commission and the US Coast Guard, resulted in the British Government ordering 25 for joint RN/RAF use.

In 1943, a small number of RN pilots were sent to the USA to learn the principles of rotary wing flying, and on their return a Flight was formed equipped with Sikorsky R-4s. The Flight's task was to carry out communication, photographic and radar calibration duties. On 7 May 1947, this Flight was formed into 705 Squadron, RNAS Gosport. Although the original tasks were retained, limited pilot training was added. On 1 February 1947, Lieutenant K. M. Reed made the first helicopter landing on a battleship, when he put his Gadfly – the naval name for the R-4 – down on the forecastle of HMS *Vanguard*, off Portland.

Search and Rescue

It was now accepted that the first operational role for helicopters in the RN was to be air-sea rescue, in place of the amphibian Sea Otter. The Admiralty fully recognized the helicopter's importance in A/S work and only waited a suitable design with the ability to carry a weapon fit. The R-4 had no such capability.

Hoverfly FT833 was one of some 50 which served with 771 Fleet Requirements Unit at Portland and with 705 Squadron, Gosport. It had a 180-hp engine, top speed of 82 mph (70 knots), rotor diameter 38 ft (11.5 m) and length 35 ft 3 in (10.5 m).

In May, 705 was equipped with Sikorsky R-4Bs, now known as the Hoverfly, and also had two R-6s. Early in 1947, Westland acquired a licence to build the Sikorsky S51 and these variants, with the more powerful 520-hp Alvis Leonides engine in place of the Pratt and Whitney Wasp Junior, were called Dragonflies. Top speed was about 103 mph (89 knots). The Mk1 made its first flight in 1948 and in January 1950, 705 was re-equipped with the Dragonfly (below). The squadron's task was to train pilots for detached SAR Flights in carriers or on Naval Air Stations.

As the Hoverfly pioneered small deck landing, merchant ship A/S operations and gave the RN its only helicopter operational practice for four years, so the Dragonfly pioneered the techniques of air-sea rescue and the training of new crews. Each aircraft carrier was equipped with two as were major Naval Air Stations. The Mk1s had a hydraulic winch. These helicopters with rotor blades of composite construction covered with fabric, gave way to the Mk3s with metal blades, of which 60 were built for the RN. This made 705 the only operational helicopter squadron in the world, outside of America.

Early in 1951, a Dragonfly carried out deck-landing trials on the RFA *Fort Duquesne*, using a small platform built on the after-structure. This proved conclusively that, in an emergency, merchant ships could be converted to helicopter carriers. Early in 1951, the first Dragonfly to go to sea for SAR duties embarked in HMS *Indomitable*. The unit was commanded by Commissioned Pilot Doug Elliott.

After US helicopters had proved their operational value during the early part of the Korean War, the USS *Phillipine Sea* lent a helicopter to HMS *Theseus*. The helicopter and crew were transferred on 3 April 1951, and on 12 April – when a Firefly piloted by Commissioned Pilot F. D. Bailey was damaged by flak and landed in the sea 40 miles from the *Theseus* – Bailey was rescued by the helicopter lent to the *Theseus*. This was possibly the first rescue at sea by a helicopter operated from a British carrier.

Improvisation was the key word in British SAR operations as no equipment had been standard issue. The standard strop was designed by Chief Petty Officer S. W. Lock, Ship Flight, HMS *Theseus*, in the middle of 1953. On 4 August, Lieutenant W. Davis, DSC, ditched in a Sea Fury from the *Theseus* and was rescued by Lieutenant-Commander B. Harris and CPO Lock.

It was a combination of gales, wind and tides which produced the disastrous floods on the night of 31 January/1 February 1953, when the sea defences collapsed on the east coast of Britain and the Zeeland areas of Holland and rendered thousands of people homeless. Some 1,600 people were drowned in both countries, together with cattle, sheep and dogs, and communications were disrupted. This disaster gave the RN 'choppers' a real chance to show their paces and the 9 Dragonflies of 705 flew to Holland and in 2½ weeks rescued 810 survivors. One machine made history by carrying 7 people in what was one of the biggest rescue operations ever carried out by helicopters.

The helicopter had indeed arrived, for at the Coronation Review in June 1953 12 Dragonflies flew at the head of the massed Naval Air Squadrons.

The Dragonfly was fitted with a pilot-operated winch with worm-gearing, which weighed 25-cwt (1,273 kg), was 70 ft (21 m) long and could carry a maximum load of 380-lb (173 kg). Initially there was no inter-communication facility between pilot and winchman.

Within a few months of the Dragonfly entering service, Westlands said they would build the eight-seater S55; the first one (G-AMJT) flew in November 1952. It was acquired by the RN for evaluation and following successful trials in which it proved superior to the Dragonfly in every role, an initial order was placed for a naval variant to be known as the Whirlwind HAR1.

The first production models again went to 705 Squadron, but they were not the first to operate Whirlwinds. In November 1952, the RN had taken delivery of 20 American-built HAR21s and these equipped the first operational squadron, 848, which saw active service in Malaya from March 1953, during the insurgency operations.

HAR21s and HAS22s were similar in appearance to the HAR3 XJ396 above. The HAR5 below was the first with a British power plant and a horizontal instead of anhedral tail stabilizer.

The Whirlwind could tow a paravane for minesweeping in addition to its other functions in SAR. The series 1 was powered by a 600-bhp Pratt and Whitney and the second naval version, the HAR3, with a 700-bhp Wright Cyclone. The series 2 had the more powerful 750-bhp Alvis Leonides Major, and finally, in the middle of 1966 came the HAR9, the conversion powered by a Bristol Siddeley Gnome free turbine, with a top speed of 104 mph (168 km/h). This was another outstanding development by Westlands in the development of helicopters. The lighter, smaller and quieter engines gave reduced vibration, better performance at high altitude and opened the way to multiple-engined helicopters with an improved operational performance.

A feature of the engine installation was an automatic control which varied the power output to maintain selected rpm irrespective of the collective pitch setting.

The Whirlwind HAR9 of the Royal Navy's ice patrol ship HMS
Endurance is seen here in the Neumayer Channel, Grahamland,
February 1975.

The early Whirlwinds had a similar winch to that fitted in the
Dragonfly, fitted to a boom which was too low and made it difficult to
get the rescued person inboard. Lt-Cdr J. S. Sproule designed a raised
boom making it easier for the 'victim' to be swung into the cabin,
without traversing the boom. Later versions were fitted with a
removable package hoist to facilitate transfer between the A/S and SAR
roles. This hoist was electrically operated with a 20-cwt (1,018 kg),
64-ft (20 m) long hoist, with a maximum load of 450 lb (205 kg).

The later Whirlwind 7s and 9s could also be fitted with a 'Heave-Ho'
hand-operated hoist with a 1:4 advantage and a maximum load of
300 lb (136 kg). The original version was designed by Sproule when in
700H Flight, during the Whirlwind 7 trials of 1957.

At RNAS Ford in 1953, assisted by CPO Lock, the Sproule Net was
designed, primarily as a device for recovering dead bodies from the sea.
After tests, it became a very practicable device for recovering disabled
persons and was transferred to the Double-Lift Harness, designed in
1953 by Lieutenant-Commanders Miller and Hart and Commissioned
Observer J. Lambert. Sproule and Lock used the net for the first time
on 8 March 1955 when they recovered Lieutenant-Commander
Foulkes from the water, after he had ditched in a Firefly off
Littlehampton.

Night rescue operations, using a powerful Harley landing-light and
sea-marker flares, were abandoned on 2 December 1957 when Sproule
and Lt M. Simpson had an accident and fell into the Solent. It was decided that the unstabilized Whirlwind, without a doppler, radio altimeter and hover coupler, was unsuitable for night rescue operations.

A Westland HAS1 production helicopter XM329 during flying trials with flotation units developed under a Ministry of Aviation contract, showing the feasibility of an amphibious helicopter.

This Wessex HAS3 with the dunking sonar ready for lowering is XT256, one of three built as Mk3s from the start and was with 814 Squadron in 1967.

The prototype Wessex 1 first flew on 17 May 1957 and was powered by a Napier Gazelle gas turbine engine of 1,450 shp, a top speed of 132 mph (115 knots) and a range of 340 n. miles (390 miles, 630 km). It was fitted with a similar hoist to that fitted in later Whirlwinds. It was a self-contained unit with hydraulic motor and epicyclic gearing, cable cutter, mechanical guide, and the 30-cwt (1,527 kg) cable was 106 ft (32 m) long with a maximum load of 600 lb (273 kg).

For the first time, the Automatic Flight System gave the Navy a helicopter with day and night capability, combining a good lift capability of some 4,000 lb (1,820 kg) with the ability to carry 16 fully equipped troops. This was followed by the Wessex 3 with an updated Gazelle of 1,600 shp and the twin-Gnome engined Wessex 5 in the Commando role.

Wessex HU5s lifting stores ashore from the Commando Carrier HMS *Albion* in September 1965.

Finally, it was announced on 7 November 1966 that approval had been given in principle to the introduction of a new large helicopter with twin Gnome engines. The Westland-built Sea King has a similar package hoist to that developed for the Wessex. The cable is, however, 245 ft (75 m) long and has a maximum load of 600 lb (273 kg). The Sea King also has a much longer range and on 3 December 1969, Lieutenant-Commander V. G. Sirrett, Squadron CO of 700 Squadron, Culdrose, with Lieutenant-Commanders R. Millsdon (engineer) and J. Flindell (observer), set up a non-stop flight endurance record of 4 hours 19 minutes 21 seconds, and covered 602 miles (970 km).

In January 1977, the frigate HMS *Arrow* was off the River Helford, Cornwall, when her Wasp helicopter became unserviceable and a Sea King XV703 from 824 Squadron flown by Lieutenant S. Hutchinson, RNAS Culdrose, lifted the Wasp XS542 and flew it back to Culdrose.

Small Ships Flights

The success of the Dragonfly in the search and rescue role led to an extension of the helicopter's use for surveying at sea. HMS *Vidal* was the first survey ship fitted with a flight-deck, about 30 ft × 50 ft (9 m × 15 m) and trials were successfully completed in 1954. The following year, the *Vidal*'s helicopter took part in the annexation of the island of Rockall. That same year, the ice patrol ship HMS *Protector* was converted for helicopter operations with a ship's Flight of two Whirlwind HAR1s.

The landing of a helicopter on a small ship poses very big problems, and in 1948 Sproule submitted an idea to the Admiralty. He suggested that four suction pads be attached to the undercarriage. These would be powered by an engine-driven vacuum pump with a pilot-operated release valve.

In 1955, while commanding the SAR Flight at RNAS Ford, Sproule developed the harpoon-grid system and a Dragonfly took part in the trials programme of March 1955. However, there was no immediate need for arrester gear in small ships and no further action was taken.

By 1957 it was obvious that if the A/S capabilities of helicopters were to be exploited to the full, Small Ship Flights must be able to operate in all conditions when A/S operations were possible. When the Naval Air Department at RAE began investigations, very little information was available and it was realized that continuous monitoring of all relevant factors would be needed – pitch and roll, relative wind speed and direction, sea state and, most importantly, motion of a ship after touch-down to give the handling party time to secure the helicopter safely.

Suction-pad trials were carried out in HMS *Undaunted* and *Ashanti* during 1961 and 1962 but were only partially successful. The pads gave good deck-securing qualities but were bad for helicopter handling. The harpoon-grid system was tested at RAE Bedford in 1960 but was abandoned and the winch-down was tried on a simulator but abandoned because helicopter control could prove too difficult.

Meanwhile, at the 1958 SBAC Show at Farnborough, Saunders-Roe introduced their P531, a small, high performance, general-purpose helicopter. The first flight of the prototype took place on 20 July 1958. It was powered by the Blackburn Turmo 600 series free turbine power plant, obviating the need for a clutch in the transmission with flexibility at constant power with different rotor speeds.

A naval variant named the Wasp was delivered to the RN for trials and evaluation. Ship trials in HMS *Undaunted* were under the general control of Commander Nigel Ball, DFC, and the flying was shared between the CO of 700 Squadron, Lieutenant-Commander R. Shilcock, and Lieutenants Fournel and Barstow. It was announced on 30 December 1959, that during the five-week trials, some 300 landings – including 30 by night – had been completed. The small platform built aft was only 21 ft × 26 ft (6 m × 8 m) and these landings were believed to be the first in a frigate by a helicopter.

Before further work was done on the harpoon system, the decision was taken to fit the Wasp with a wide-spaced, castored-wheel strengthened undercarriage. This would rely on friction alone for deck-landings. Developed with it was a tie-down centre swivel as the last point of attachment to the flight-deck. The tie could be released by the pilot and permitted the helicopter to be swivelled into the wind using the tail rotor, with the wheels set at a tangent to the landing circle. The wheel position could be altered for shore operations to give effective braking.

Initial trials in HMS *Nubian* confirmed the operational feasibility of the system, and first of class trials were completed in HMS *Leander* during February 1963.

On 28 August 1962, this Wasp XN334, fitted with the special undercarriage mentioned in the text, did landing trials in HMS *Ashanti*.

On 3 May 1960, the Saunders-Roe Wasp powered by a Gnome turbine engine made a first flight of 45 minutes at the Saunders-Roe Division of Westland Aircraft Limited. This Gnome had a 1,000-shp rating giving the Wasp first class performance at high altitude and in tropical conditions.

Finally, of course, comes the Westland Lynx, which in naval service has a wheeled undercarriage like the Wasp. The Lynx was a joint Anglo-French development with the production based in Britain by Westlands.

It is a high-speed general-purpose helicopter powered by two Rolls-Royce free turbines, to give a maximum speed of 186 mph (160 knots). It can carry 12 people and has the ability to operate from small ships in rough seas with minimum handling equipment. Folding of the tail section and main rotor blades permits stowage in small hangars. It can be fitted for SAR with a winch capable of lifting 600 lb (293 kg) to 250 ft (78 m). A central warning display indicates any malfunction of the various systems which include printed circuitry in console and instrument panels. Stainless steel, plastic honeycomb, glass-reinforced plastic and advanced engineering are included in the design.

172

Main Details

Length (rotors turning)	49 ft 9 in	(15.16 m)
Width (rotors turning)	40 ft	(12.8 m)
Height (tail rotor stopped)	11 ft 6 in	(3.51 m)
Length (folded)	34 ft 10 in	(10.62 m)
Width (folded)	9 ft 7½ in	(2.94 m)
Height (folded)	10 ft 6 in	(3.2 m)

Weight

Maximum all-up	9,100-lb	(4,128 kg)
Bare weight	5,403-lb	(2,451 kg)

Speed

Continuous cruising	150 knots	(174 mph)
Best endurance	70 knots	(82 mph)

Powered by two Rolls-Royce BS360 gas turbines, maximum rating 900-shp each. Has folding main rotor blades and tail pylon for stowage at sea, with a negative rotor pitch facility, and the harpoon-grid deck-securing system.

Anti-Submarine Role

A tremendous advantage enjoyed by submarines over surface warships has always been that their passive detection ranges are better by about 10:1, enabling early evasive action to be taken. Aerial surveillance has driven them back beneath the sea to a large extent with the detection methods based on sonobuoys, infra-red detection, magnetic anomaly detection (MAD), or dunking sonar.

The first dunking sonar used in the RN was the American low-power, short-range AN/AWS-4 with a 20-degree beam and a 360-degree search taking up to 5 minutes, including the waiting time for an echo (speed about 5,000 ft or 1,524 m a second).

On 1 March 1954, 845 Squadron commissioned as the first British A/S squadron with 8 Whirlwind HAS22 helicopters. The sonar was the American AN/AQS-4. For part of their work-up period they were in the carrier HMS *Perseus*. They used air-launched torpedoes to attack submarines and this squadron pioneered the operating procedures and tactics. The HAS Mk3 followed in November 1955 and these helicopters proved so efficient that the Admiralty ordered a special variant for the search and strike role. This was the HAS7 which flew for the first time on 17 October 1956 and was powered by the 750-bhp Alvis Leonides Major. The helicopters operated in a team of two, one with dunking sonar to detect and the other with a homing torpedo to attack. Although the Admiralty had accepted the HAS7 in the A/S role, it was now obvious that the twin search and strike roles needed a larger, more powerful aircraft, able to carry at least three crew – pilot, observer and sonar operator.

This led to the development of the Wessex HAS1, the first built entirely at Yeovil, which made its maiden flight on 20 June 1958. The automated flight control system was sophisticated for that time, and the helicopter began service trials with 700H Flight in 1960, and entered operational service in 1961. By the end of 1962, it had replaced the Whirlwind 7s as the standard A/S helicopter and the 7s took on the new role of Commando carrier with ground support duties – following the experience of 848 in Malaya.

The Wessex 1 was fitted with doppler radar navigation, radio altimeter, and auto-stabilization in roll, pitch and to a lesser extent in yaw. The Mk19 autopilot included heading and height hold, enabling the aircraft to hold plan and height above the dunking sonar. One of the major problems with the Wessex 1 was the observer's difficulty in maintaining a precise plot.

A 737 Squadron HAS1 finds a temporary home on the RFA *Tidepool* during exercise Lime Jub – no fuel problems here!

This was overcome by the Wessex 3, the first British-built helicopter fitted with all-British equipment. It had lightweight primary and secondary radars; improved doppler radar with digital computer for position; automatic tactical plotting display; improved sonar; and an improved autopilot, the AFCS 30. This latter included specialized A/S functions: airspeed hold; dunking sonar vertical hold; pictorial display flight director; mean sea level hold – to prevent following wave profile; and an improved 1,600-bhp Gazelle with an extended rotor-head fairing. The HAS3 was the first complete A/S airborne platform for the RN, and in September 1967 they replaced the Wessex 1s in 814 Squadron.

The Wessex 3 in fact exceeded most of the Navy's expectations and operational experience greatly improved the range and scope of A/S operations. Although able to operate as a self-contained tactical air unit directing A/S operations in a particular area, it was limited in scope by endurance being single-engined, and in attack capability.

The Wessex 3 XS149 pictured over the guided missile destroyer HMS *Fife*. The HAS3 is easily identified by the advanced radar system dome just behind the rotor head.

It was announced on 27 June 1966, that the Sea King SH-3D was to be introduced with twin Gnome turbine engines. It was to carry homing torpedoes, sonar, improved doppler, all-weather flight control and a powerful radar. It was the most advanced and largest helicopter ordered for any navy in the world.

A Sea King helicopter HAS1 (XV672) operating from HMS *Hermes*, prepared to lower her sonar during a submarine hunt in February 1977.

On 19 August 1969, 700S Squadron commissioned at RNAS Culdrose as the Sea King Intensive Flying Trials Squadron, and they later won the Boyd Trophy for introducing the helicopter into naval service. Sea King is a boat-hulled aircraft with sponsors and a range double that of the Wessex 3, and has electronic fuel/power computers for the Gnome turbines. The AFCS 31 has improved reliability and the helicopter can carry four homing torpedoes and has a multiple attack capability. Completely new features include a powered folding five-bladed rotor, and retractable undercarriage.

It is also of interest to note that the first deck-landing by a Sea King was made on the RFA *Engadine*, off Portland, on 2 July 1969. The first operational squadron was 824 Squadron, formed RNAS Culdrose in February 1970, and then embarked in the *Ark Royal*.

In 1974 during the Turkish invasion of Cyprus, 814 Squadron Sea Kings from the *Hermes* lifted 1,600 civilians to safety. A total of 50 Sea Kings were delivered to the RN.

The last helicopter to enter service with the Navy was the Westland Lynx. In June 1972 it broke two world class speed records and achieved a maximum of 173 mph (321 km/h). A large cabin can take up to 10 troops or 3,300 lb (1,500 kg) freight.

The ability to operate from small ships in rough seas with maximum operational capability and minimum maintenance, was of prime importance. Folding tail boom and main rotor blades permit stowage in small hangars. In the A/S role a tactical display is provided in the cabin cockpit and the Lynx can carry two homing torpedoes or other weapons. In the surface search and strike role, wire-guided missiles such as the SS11 or AS12 can be fitted and, when armed with homing missiles, the helicopter can be effective against larger surface vessels. A central warning display indicates any malfunction in the various aircraft systems.

The Intensive Flying Trials Unit was 700L Squadron, RNAS Yeovilton and 702 Squadron at Yeovilton, formed in January 1978 as the Headquarters/Training Squadron. Both operate Lynx HAS2s, and one of these helicopters from 700L formed the first operational Ship Flight in HMS *Birmingham*.

Commando and Support Roles

The versatility and scope of the helicopter in naval or commando service is wide and varied. It has been from the very start.

A Wessex 5 helps out during the dry season in Hong Kong, using a specially adapted water carrier for fire fighting.

They first went on active service in Malaya with 848 Squadron operating Whirlwind HAR21s and did not withdraw until three years later. They ferried troops round the jungle areas and were used in rescue work, medical evacuation and general ground support duties. A very high standard of flying was required in meeting adverse weather conditions, flying over featureless jungles without navigational facilities and in rescue work. These operations led to the build-up of the only Naval Air Station outside the UK, RNAS Sembawang, HMS *Simbang*, a few miles from Singapore. It was here that helicopter facilities for the Far East Fleet were provided and was, at the time, the only Naval Air Station to be commanded by a Royal Marine officer, when home for 42 Commando, HQ 3 Brigade, Royal Marines, 40 Commando, and 95 Light Commando Regiment, RA, which was attached to the 3rd Brigade.

Originally intended as a bomber station for the RAF, Sembawang was carved out of a rubber estate in 1937 but was transferred to the Admiralty in 1939 and plans were made to convert it to a major RNAS and repair yard, to support a projected FE Fleet with up to four Fleet carriers. On the outbreak of war, it was transferred to the RAAF. In September 1945, when the occupation by the Japanese ended, a naval advance party under Captain H. A. Trail took over. The following October, the station commissioned as HMS *Simbang*.

During the Malaya emergency and the Indonesian confrontation, FAA helicopters operated throughout the area and maintained a high degree of serviceability despite intensive flying in some of the world's worst conditions.

After the quelling of the Brunei Revolt, 845 Squadron, which operated from *Albion* and then *Bulwark*, flew thousands of hours in support of the Army. They also carried out scores of medical evacuations for the local Ibans. For their services, 845 Squadron were awarded the Boyd Trophy, the Fleet Air Arm's top award.

848 Squadron spent nearly two years operating Whirlwinds in Borneo, and for a small party of British soldiers manning a radio relay station on top of an 8,000-ft mountain in Sarawak, Malaysian Borneo, the FAA Wessex helicopters of 848 were their only link with the outside world. The mountain top was covered in cloud nearly all the time and the weather was so cold – yes cold – that the signallers wore special warm clothing. Conditions were so bad that there was perhaps only an hour or so a day when a helicopter could land on the small pad hacked out of the mountain. 848 also helped open up the jungle interior of Sabah and provided valuable support to a Royal Australian Engineer troop.

After four years of intensive operational flying in the Borneo States, the last FAA helicopters pulled out in 1966, a detachment of Wessex 5s from 845 Naval Air Commando Squadron embarking in the *Bulwark* for Australia.

Flight of Wessex 5 helicopters from 845 Squadron with XT455 nearest camera.

Aerial view of the Commando Carrier HMS *Bulwark*, with lift wells clearly visible, being re-stored by the RFA *Regent*.

During June 1964, Wessex helicopters of 815 Squadron alone performed the important task of supplying troops in the Radfan mountains, Aden. Commanded by Lieutenant-Commander John Bluett, they flew 427 sorties, carried 1,300 passengers, and lifted 160,000 lb (72,700 kg) of freight. They made daily nightmare landings on mountainsides and tops in this stark and barren land, often flying 8 hours a day.

A Wessex 5 moves in to pick up a gun in hilly countryside, a typical example of the way in which helicopters give mobility and flexibility to Commandos or troops.

In the search and rescue role, the holiday season each year from April to September is always a busy time for naval helicopters. In 1966 for instance at RNAS Culdrose, on the east coast of Cornwall, SAR helicopters made 27 sorties involving the recovery of 16 people involved in swimming, sailing, boating or cliff-climbing accidents. The first major SAR attempt was by Dragonfly helicopters trying to rescue people from the submarine HMS *Affray* in September 1951, followed by the Flying Enterprise incident in January 1952.

In July 1952, Lieutenant R. Seymour flew his Wasp helicopter from HMS *Yarmouth* through a storm to the *Oriental Falcon* 25 miles away. Despite an electrical fault which put his landing light out and in a force 7 gale, 13 seamen were winched to safety in 4 sorties lasting 2 hours 30 minutes. The *Yarmouth* sailed for Hong Kong, but two days later received a second SOS call from the 20 crew who had elected to stay with the ship. In hazardous conditions, Lt Seymour and his crew carried out this rescue too, and he was awarded the Air Force Cross for "... a very high degree of flying skill and personal courage, combined with excellent judgement."

On 7 October 1971, the US cargo ship *Steel Vendor* foundered in the South China Sea and two Sea King helicopters of 826 Squadron, HMS *Eagle*, flew off to give assistance. Typhoon Elaine had passed through the area and weather conditions were bad with heavy swells, a gusting wind up to 40 knots and swirling rain which, at times, reduced visibility to 500 yards. The cloud base was 200 ft. After flying 55 miles they found the ship listing badly. The Master informed a Squadron officer who had been winched down that the vessel was breaking up and he wanted to abandon ship. Two more Sea Kings were launched and, despite bad obstructions caused by masts and derricks, the weather and continual movement of the ship, the crew of 40 were safely on board the *Eagle* in 2 hours 10 minutes. This magnificent rescue gained the Boyd Trophy for 1971.

The incredible *Merc Enterprise* saga began when the Danish vessel capsized in a terrifying storm 30 miles off Plymouth. Winds gusted to over 80 knots and there were 50-ft waves. Five Sea Kings from 706 Squadron, RNAS Culdrose, found the crew of 16 and 3 women in the water alongside the vessel. The helicopters had been scrambled from the hangars as conditions were so appalling. They snatched 7 seamen to safety and recovered 5 bodies. Lieutenant-Commander David Mallock and Lieutenant Antony Baker were awarded the AFC; Petty Officers David Fowles, David Jackson, and Aircrewman Adrian Williams, the Air Force Medal.

The Commando role began almost by accident when, in 1952, the Army asked the RAF for helicopters to provide communications and medical evacuations in Malaya. The RAF could not spare any helicopters and the Navy offered to provide the facility with the Whirlwind 3s and 22s recently used by 706 Squadron in the A/S role. They became 848 Squadron, arrived at Singapore in HMS *Perseus* on 8 January 1953, and were operational two weeks later.

The experience of 848 gave the Army a mobility and flexibility never experienced before and the Royal Marines and RN discussed the best ship to use for these operations. The Suez landings in 1956 provided an opportunity to confirm the operational decisions reached. Two Light Fleet carriers, the *Ocean* and *Theseus*, carried in the first wave of 45 Commando at dawn. In 90 minutes they landed 415 men and 23 tons of stores. They lost three helicopters.

As a result, the Light Fleet carrier HMS *Bulwark* was converted to the Commando role, and in January 1958 the Amphibious Warfare Trials Unit was formed and transferred to Malta to operate there with the Royal Marines. Primary tasks were ferrying troops, stores and ammunition, artillery spotting, casualty evacuation and reconnaissance. The development of basic night and instrument flying techniques started in March 1958.

Bulwark from above showing the operating positions for the nine helicopters which can be ranged on deck at any one time, and the general layout.

These early evaluation trials confirmed the importance of the Commando concept and led to the specialized ships and helicopters as we know them today. On 19 January 1960, the *Bulwark* recommissioned as a Commando Carrier and HMS *Albion* started a two-year conversion to one. On 1 August 1962, the *Albion* commissioned as a Commando Carrier.

The *Albion* RO7 and the *Bulwark* RO8 were modified Centaur Class carriers, displacing 27,000 ton full load, 737 ft o.a., 123 ft extreme beam and 27 ft draught. Powered by Parsons geared turbines, their twin screws gave them a speed of 29.5 knots on trials. They cost £9–£10 million originally, had a crew of 1,037 and accommodation for 600 Commandos.

With the Navy's ever-increasing use of helicopters, it was announced in July 1973 that the Aircrewman Branch of the FAA was to be reformed. It had lapsed after the end of the Second World War because of the limited numbers required.

Bulwark scrambles her RM Commando in Wessex helicopters during an exercise assault on Gibraltar in 'Rock Climb', August 1969.

A demonstration of 41 Commando embarking in the Wessex 5 helicopters of 848 Squadron, operating from the Commando Carrier HMS *Albion*.

Featured above is a Wessex 5 XS479 (the first production aircraft) operating from an improvised landing pad in the jungle and, below, another Wessex 5 in snow camouflage supporting ground operations. These pictures highlight the versatility of the helicopter, and although there was difficulty with operations in extreme sub-zero temperatures early on, these have now been largely overcome. RAE Farnborough have been experimenting with a de-icing paste.

847 Squadron Wessex 5s are pictured below over the town of Singapore and, top right, overflying the harbour. Bottom right: another Wessex over the wreck of the tanker *Torrey Canyon*.

This photograph shows clearly the take-off sequence of commando-carrying helicopters from the *Albion*. The Wessex HU5s could go into action carrying a dozen fully armed Commandos with bulky loads slung beneath the aircraft and released from the hover. It could also go into action against ground targets with missiles or as a 'gun ship'.

On 1 September 1968, Rear-Admiral M. F. Fell, DSO, DSC, (then
Flag Officer Aircraft Carriers) assumed responsibility for amphibious
matters formerly exercised by Commander Far East Fleet and C-in-C
Plymouth. He became the first Flag Officer Carriers and Amphibious
Ships (FOCAS) – the carriers *Albion*, *Bulwark*, and the Headquarters
Assault Ships *Fearless* (pictured below) and *Intrepid*. *Fearless* and
Intrepid had a rear dock which could be flooded and the stern gate
lowered to allow assault landing craft to sail out fully laden with troops
or equipment.

The Gazelle helicopter replaced the Hiller 12E and the Whirlwind HAS7 in the training role and was part of the 1967 joint Anglo-French collaborative helicopter programme. The first of 30 for the Navy first flew in 1973, and production aircraft (like XW853 shown here) went to RNAS Culdrose on 10 December 1974, and from March 1975 formed 705 Squadron. Basically a development of the Alouette, 9 of them flew during the Queen's Review of the Fleet at Spithead on 28 June 1977, 6 from 705 and 3 from the Royal Marines.

The multi-role utility and training helicopter, with a crew of two, can carry up to three passengers, and has a service ceiling of 16,400 ft (5,000 m). It is powered by a Turbomeca Astazou turbo-shaft engine of 592 shp, giving a cruising speed of 164 mph (143 knots) and a maximum speed of 192 mph (166 knots). It has a maximum range of 416 miles (666 kms) or a normal range of 225 miles (360 kms) with a 1,100 lb (500 kgs) payload. It can be armed with a wide variety of weapons including AS11 or AS12 missiles, 36-mm rocket pods, two forward firing or a single cabin-mounted 7.62 machine-gun. The rotor diameter is 34 ft 5½ in (10.5 m), overall length 39 ft 3¼ in (12 m), and overall height is 10 ft 2½ in (3 m).

It is one of several Westland/Aerospatiale models built under a joint production agreement signed in 1967.

The other Westland models mentioned in this chapter were manufactured under licence from Sikorski, with a joint agreement signed in 1946, beginning with the S-51, S-55 and other later models. In 1959, Westland took over the Saunders-Roe Helicopter Division, and in 1960, the rotary wing divisions of the Fairey and Bristol companies.

In 1977/1978 it was stated that the Fleet Air Arm had 174 fixed-wing aircraft and 341 helicopters. Strength and disposition as follows:

Establishment Ship	Squadron	Aircraft
HMS *Ark Royal*	809	Buccaneer S2
	824	Sea King HAS2
	849 B Flight	Gannet AEW3
	892	Phantom FG1
	SAR Flight	2 Wessex HAR1
HMS *Hermes*	814	Sea King HAS2
	845	Wessex HU5
	846	Wessex HU5
County Class Destroyers	737	Wessex HAS3
	820	Sea King HAS2
	826	Sea King HAS2
ASW Frigates/Destroyers	829	40 Wasp HAS1
RNAS Culdrose	705	Gazelle HT2 training
	706	Sea King HAS1 training
	750	Sea Prince C Mk1 communications
	771	Wessex HAS1 training
RNAS Lee-on-Solent	781	Sea Devon, Sea Heron, Wessex, Chipmunk, training and communications
Prestwick	819	Sea King HAS2
RNAS Yeovilton	702	Lynx HAS2 training
RNAS Yeovilton	702	Lynx HAS2 training
	707	Wessex HU5 training

The 1979/1980 strength was given as follows:

Establishment/Ship	Aircraft	Number of Squadrons	Number of Flights
HMS *Hermes*	Sea King HAS2	1	
HMS *Bulwark*	Sea King HAS2	1	
HMS *Blake*	Sea King HAS2	1	
RFAs	Sea King HAS2	1	
Prestwick	Sea King HAS2	1	
RNAS Culdrose	Sea King HAS2	1 training	
Leanders, Type 42 Destroyers and Type 21 Frigates	Lynx HAS2		13
Leander, Rothesay, Tribal Class frigates; Type 42 and Type 21	Wasp		31
RNAS Portland	Wasp	1 training	
County Class Destroyers	Wessex HAS3		5
RNAS Portland	Wessex HAS3	2 training	
RNAS Yeovilton	Wessex HU5	2 commando 1 training	
RNAS Portland FRU	Wessex HU5	1	

On 18 November 1938, the Air Branch of the RNVR was formed and by 1954 its personnel operated about a third of all FAA aircraft. It was disbanded in 1957 because of Defence cuts.

On 9 November 1979, it was announced at the annual dinner of the RNVR Association at RNC Greenwich, that an Air Reserve of the RNR was to be introduced. It would be restricted to ex-FAA personnel under 38, who had left the Service not more than five years previously, with a retirement age of 50.

The object of the Air Reserve was to augment front-line squadrons and provide a limited pool of professional aircrew for communications, naval control of shipping, mine counter-measures and support roles, flying fixed wing aircraft or helicopters. It was hoped that 40 officers would start training in 1980 with a maximum of 60 by 1982/3.

CARRIERS AND COMMANDO SHIPS

Ordered on 19 May 1942 as part of the Fleet Carrier War Construction Programme, HMS *Eagle* was launched on 19 March 1946 by the Queen (then Princess Elizabeth) and completed on 10 October 1951. The *Eagle* was accepted into service on 1 March 1952.

Built by Vickers Armstrong Ltd, she was begun as the *Audacious* but was renamed the *Eagle* on 21 January 1946. The original cost was £15,795,000. After seven years' optional service, she was taken in hand for a major refit costing £31 million and taking from 1959–1964. HMS *Eagle* emerged with a new outline as the most modern carrier in the world. She had an 8½° angled flight-deck, fitted for the first time in any British carrier along the axis of the flight-deck, together with improved lighting to assist night landings. Displacing 50,000 ton (revised estimate), her flight-deck was 803 ft long (245 m), and her beam was 166 ft o.a. (51 m). Parsons geared turbines with four shafts gave her a speed of 31.5 knots and she was armed with six quadruple Seacat launchers, eight 4.5-inch guns, four 3-pounders and carried 42 aircraft – Buccaneer, Sea Vixen, Gannet AEW3 and Wessex helicopters for A/S and SAR duties, Maximum complement was 2,750.

The *Eagle* with her aircraft ranged on deck.

A Buccaneer of 800 Squadron from the *Eagle* is shown on patrol over the Aden/Khormatisar airfield during the withdrawal of British troops 29 November 1967.

A Buccaneer S1 lands on the carrier carefully watched by the plane-guard helicopter, hovering just to port of the flight-deck, in case of a 'ditching'.

It was claimed for the *Victorious* when she recommissioned with the first ship-borne 3-D radar, that it was the most successful air defence system ever fitted in a Britain warship. History was repeated in 1964 when the *Eagle* recommissioned in May with the same computer-operated system at the heart of which was Poseidon, a new digital computer capable of doing the job previously carried out by 60 men in the *Victorious*. The system could handle 500,000 addition or subtractions a second with an accuracy of one part in 16 millions. This computer brought a tremendous improvement in the speed of decision taking and the efficiency of air defence systems.

Mention must also be made of the new Integrated Communications System fitted, which was developed by the Royal Navy Scientific Service. A warship has many problems not experienced ashore due to the close siting of transmitting and receiving aerials.

When the *Eagle* rejoined the Fleet her Captain was Leslie Derek Empson who joined the RN as a Naval Airman second class and served with 812 Squadron in the last *Eagle* during the war. It was the first time an ex-RNVR pilot had become captain of an aircraft carrier. Other famous captains have included J. D. Treacher who handed over command to I. G. Robertson, and on promotion to Flag Rank relieved Mike Fell as FONAC. Captain Treacher was in command when two Harrier V/STOL aircraft landed in *Eagle* during 1970.

The *Ark Royal* (left) and the *Eagle* pictured during joint exercises in 1970.

197

A Sea Vixen catapults off the flight-deck of the *Eagle* closely watched by the rescue helicopter. Seen below is the *Ark Royal* passing *Eagle* for the last time on 5 April 1978.

The *Eagle* was destored during 1972 and was finally placed on the disposal list at Plymouth.

HMS *Centaur*, RO6, was a Light Fleet Carrier laid down on 30 May 1944, launched 22 April 1947 and completed on 1 September 1953; she cost £10,434,000. Of some 27,000 ton full load, improvements were incorporated in her building, giving her an interim angled flight-deck of 5½° with five arrester wires, and her speed was boosted to 29.5 knots.

During 1957 she was equipped with new arrester gear and steam catapults during a refit which lasted until March 1961. She was 737 ft o.a. (225 m), with a beam of 123 ft (38 m) and could operate up to 45 aircraft, including a squadron of helicopters. Accommodation was provided for a maximum of 1,390 officers and men including aircrew.

The man behind the camera obviously had an eye for detail and composition. This impressive picture was taken on board the *Centaur* by Admiral Sir John Hamilton, KBE, CB, when Commander-in-Chief Mediterranean. The White Ensign and the Admiral's Flag complete the picture. Taken in December 1965 with a Super Ikonta, Tessa 3.5 lens, F11 at 1/125, yellow filter on FP3 film.

The Commando Carrier HMS *Albion* arrived in Plymouth on 22 November 1973 after her fifth and last commission which had taken her to 21 ports in 15 countries, in just 23 months. Two days later she left for her home port of Portsmouth to end a career which had spanned 18 years of naval aviation history.

She had been laid down on 23 March 1944 and launched on 6 May 1947 by Mrs Clement Attlee. Work stopped on her until 1949 and she was finally accepted into service as a Light Fleet Carrier in October 1954. She recommissioned on 26 June 1956 and her Sea Hawks flew the first rocket strikes against the Egyptian forces during the Suez landings, and the light fleet carriers *Ocean* and *Theseus* operated helicopters to put 45 Commando ashore.

Operating as a single-seat fighter without drop tanks or bombs, the Sea Hawk had a top speed of 560 mph (485 knots) at 36,000 ft (10,975 m), and with an initial rate of climb of 5,700 ft/min (1,738 m/min), could reach her service ceiling of 44,500 ft (13,570 m) in 12 minutes. Operational radius of action was 288 miles (460 km).

Built by the Coventry firm of Armstrong Whitworth with a skin of stressed metal, Sea Hawks had a production run of 434 aircraft with the last (XE 490) delivered in 1956. These aircraft equipped 13 front-line squadrons, and later went to 1832, 1835 and 1836 squadrons RNVR, and to some second-line units. An aerobatic team from 738 Training Squadron performed at the SBAC Show, Farnborough, in 1957. Sea Hawks were superseded by Scimitars in front-line service.

848 Squadron overflying the *Albion* during her work-up, February 1965.

    The *Albion* had done four commissions as a fixed-wing carrier before starting a two-year conversion in 1960 and she recommissioned as a Commando Carrier on 1 August 1962. The same year she was active at Brunei, Sarawak, and during 1964 in East Africa. This was followed by intensive helicopter operations in Malaysia during the confrontation with Indonesia. After a winter refit in 1968, she relieved the *Bulwark* in Aden, operating in support of 42 Commando ashore, who finally withdrew to the *Albion* on 29 November.

A closer look at a formation of 848 Wessex 5s over the ship.

The inevitable Russian snooper follows the *Albion* during exercise 'Dawn Patrol 72' in the Mediterranean.

The *Albion* (Captain J. H. Adams, MVO) sailed for the Far East from Portsmouth at the start of her second commission as a Commando Carrier, on 12 March 1965. Wessex 5s of 848 Squadron (Lieutenant-Commander G. A. Andrews) flew on board, together with Sioux helicopters of 40 Commando Air Troop.

On completing a further refit on 20 March 1970, she was commanded by Captain C. H. Leach. He was relieved on 2 June 1972 by Captain W. D. M. Staveley. For her fifth and last commission, she was commanded by Captain J. G. Jungius.

The *Albion* off Singapore during 1971.

HMS *Bulwark* was originally designed as a Light Fleet Carrier of the Centaur Class and was laid down 10 May 1945. Launched 22 June 1948, she was completed on 4 June 1954. During this first commission, the carrier took part in the Suez landings and her three squadrons of Sea Hawks, 804, 810, and 895, virtually destroyed the Egyptian Air Force on the ground and gave close support to the first-ever helicopter landings of Commando Forces. During conversion to the first Commando Carrier for the Royal Navy at Portsmouth in 1959, arrester wires and catapults were removed, and eighteen 40 mm anti-aircraft guns were removed to make room for four sponsons each carrying an assault landing craft. She recommissioned on 19 January 1960 to support the Strike Carriers *Ark Royal*, *Centaur* and *Hermes* then in commission. In addition to a crew of 950, she could carry a full Commando and operated up to 20 helicopters, able to airlift men or vehicles ashore. At short notice using their own resources, technicians could convert the helicopters to the A/S role.

Contrary to many popular newspaper reports, the *Bulwark* was not moth-balled but was placed in Reserve in April 1976 and re-activated in late 1977. In 1981, due to the economic situation, the *Bulwark* was withdrawn from service some six months earlier than expected, and placed on the disposal list.

During the *Bulwark's* visit to Fort Lauderdale with 848 Squadron and 40 Commando embarked, three Wessex helicopters staged a ceremonial flypast streaming the Union Jack, the White Ensign and the Stars and Stripes. This was a rehearsal for the US bicentennial celebrations.

In January 1975 in the South China Sea, the *Bulwark* and HMS *Berwick* are shown being refuelled by the RFA *Tidesurge*.

The ceremonial flypast as it actually happened in March 1976 at a height of 150 ft (46 m). Led by Lieutenant-Commander Jeremy Knapp (CO 848), they streamed the Bicentennial Jack as well (nearest camera) which was being flown by all USN ships. In the background a private aircraft streams a banner welcoming the *Bulwark*.

HMS *Victorious* – The Mighty Vic – was built by Vickers Armstrong at Walker-on-Tyne and was launched on 14 September 1939. She completed on 15 May 1941 and despite not having finished her proper trials, set out a month later and found the elusive *Bismarck*. Her aircraft scored a torpedo hit and a probable, and contributed towards the final destruction of this mighty battleship.

On 10 August, the *Victorious* (Captain H. C. Bovell), with the *Indomitable* (Captain T. H. Troubridge) and the *Eagle* (Captain L. D. Mackintosh) sailed from Gibraltar with the Pedestal Convoy for the relief of Malta. (The author was in HMS *Sirius*.) The following day, while turning to fly off aircraft, the *Eagle* was torpedoed and sunk with heavy loss of life. The *Furious* was ferrying aircraft with the convoy and the *Argus* was at Gibraltar with replacement aircraft.

During Operation Torch, the allied invasion of North Africa, the *Victorious* operated with HMS *Illustrious*, *Formidable*, *Argus*, *Biter*, *Dasher*, *Avenger* and *Archer*. On 8 November, Lieutenant B. H. C. Nation, leading a section of four Martlets from the *Victorious*, landed alone at Blida Airfield and received its surrender.

Watched by an interested body of naval airmen, more used to jet fighters and heavier aircraft, an Army Auster AOP9 demonstrates its expertise in a STOL landing without an arrester hook, on the *Victorious*.

Above, Commander E. R. Anson, CO of 801 Squadron, makes his last sortie in a Buccaneer S1 before relinquishing command of the squadron, when *Victorious* was in the Far East, April 1964. Seen below is another S1 with the famous 'V' symbol lining up before take-off. A Wessex 1 plane-guard hovers nearby.

Between 1950–1958, the *Victorious* was modernized in Portsmouth Dockyard with her displacement increased to 35,500 ton. She was floated out of dry-dock on 19 May 1955. The programme which made her the world's most modern carrier, included the fitting of a fully angled flight-deck of 8¾°, mirror landing-sights, high-speed lifts, and two parallel track catapults 145 ft long (44 m) with blast deflectors. The 775 ft long (236 m) flight-deck was strengthened to take the heaviest aircraft, and the arresting gear consisted of four wires with an average space of 80 ft (24 m).

She recommissioned on 14 January 1958 and during a year east of Suez in 1960, spent 222 days out of 333 at sea, steaming 83,000 miles.

With Victoria Peak in the background, and a Chinese junk and a ferry steamer in the foreground, the *Victorious* is seen in Hong Kong.

The unmistakable outline of the Gannet's Double Mamba and twin propellers form the lead-in for this photograph showing activities on deck as the *Victorious* approached Kuwait.

With her Scimitars (foreground), Sea Vixen FAW1s and Gannet aircraft ranged on deck, the *Victorious* leaves Singapore for Hong Kong in September 1961.

The *Victorious* leaves Hong Kong with the Ship's Crest beautifully portrayed forward and some aircraft on deck.

211

A further refit followed which allowed her to operate the Buccaneers, and she returned to the Far East in 1963.

The last historic moment for the 'Mighty Vic' followed a disastrous fire on 23 November 1967, after which it was announced she would not recommission. HMS *Victorious* formally ended her career on 13 March 1968. When she left Portsmouth for the last time to be towed to a Scottish shipbreakers, Vice-Admiral Sir Richard Janvrin flew over her in salute in the only remaining operational Swordfish, piloted by Lieutenant-Commander E. J. Trounson. Sir Richard had previously commanded the *Victorious*, and later flew his flag in her as Flag Officer Aircraft Carriers.

The Air Operations Room showing (foreground) air raid reporting officers with two tote-keepers in the same row and, beyond, intercept officer and assistant.

On her way to the scrap yard in 1969, the *Victorious* is saluted by the last flying Swordfish LS326 which is maintained in flying trim by RNAS Yeovilton. The famous 'Stringbag' could be ditched safely, pulled off the deck in a climbing turn at 55 knots and it spanned a period of nine years in operational service.

This aircraft was acquired by the Navy in 1960 and to keep it flying, was refitted with a Pegasus engine removed from the Swordfish exhibit at the Imperial War Museum. A spare non-serviceable engine was refitted in the exhibit so that its appearance was not marred. The work was supervised by Lt-Cdr R. Evans and was carried out by Chief Air Fitter Chris Forbes and Leading Air Mechanic 'Red' Readwin.

The Swordfish is painted in the original colours with the code 5A, an exact replica of the lead aircraft flown by Lt-Cdr T. P. Coode on 26 May 1941, when he led 15 Swordfish from HMS *Ark Royal*, in the attack on the German battleship *Bismarck*. The battleship was hit by three torpedoes and her steering gear was damaged, allowing the British Fleet to catch up with, and destroy her.

The Light Fleet Carrier HMS *Hermes*, the first all-missile ship to join the Fleet, was built by Vickers Limited at Barrow and was launched by Mrs Winston Churchill on 16 February 1953. She was redesigned before completion to include the most modern techniques for operating aircraft, with a 6½° angled flight-deck, steam catapults, deck edge lift, mirror landing-sight and the Type 984 radar. There was remote control of engine and boiler rooms and an enclosed citadel, allowing the carrier to operate in nuclear fall-out conditions.

She commissioned for trials on 23 October 1959, was accepted on 18 November 1959 and commissioned on 25 November 1959. She joined the Fleet during the summer of 1960, capable of operating up to 45 aircraft. She displaced 27,800 ton full load, was 744 ft o.a. (227 m) and had a beam of 153 ft (57 m). In 1966 she was modified to operate the latest strike aircraft of 801 Squadron (Buccaneers Mk2) and 893 Squadron (Sea Vixen 2 all-weather fighters). The Vixens were armed with Firestreak and Red Top air-to-air guided missiles, bombs or rockets, and had a nuclear capability.

Furious jet activity on board an aircraft carrier is common enough, but these gentle jets of HMS *Hermes* make a tranquil and picturesque contrast. This array of water jets in a pre-wetting exercise, shows how exterior surfaces can be washed down to free them from the effects of nuclear fall-out, as might occur on the fringe of a nuclear explosion.

HMS *Hermes* as she was in November 1959, during her work-up trials, before her aircraft flew on board and she joined the Fleet operationally.

A Sea Vixen, armed with Bullpup missiles, about to be launched.

Her Westland Gannet AEW3s – the flying radar sets for long-range airborne warning – were operated by 848 Squadron. The Wessex 3s with dipping sonar and homing torpedoes were operated by 814 Squadron and Wessex 1s were carried for SAR duties.

The *Hermes* had a crew of 1,900 and was fully air-conditioned with all 'mod. cons' including separate galley and dining-rooms, fresh bread and confectionery daily from a modern galley, a medical centre with consulting and operating rooms, dental surgery, a large and efficient Chinese laundry, and tailors and shoemakers providing a fast and efficient service for all.

A Buccaneer pilot in oxygen mask, radio mike and parachute harness, before a sortie from the *Hermes*.

Here she is seen leaving Singapore for the last time in February 1969, before returning to the UK via West Australia, and (below), a pre-production Buccaneer doing trials in the *Hermes*.

Scimitar jet fighters displayed in *Hermes'* 'shop window' during an exercise in July 1961. The complex radar and electronic sensors illustrated, would have put the aircraft on display in the Air Operations Room a long time before.

Her catapult days finished at Devonport Dockyard in 1970 when she was taken in hand for conversion to a Commando Carrier. She rejoined the Fleet in this role after recommissioning on 21 July 1973, exactly 60 years after Commander C. R. Samson flew the first aircraft with folding wings, the Short Folder No. 81, from the forward platform of the eighth *Hermes* – a 5,600-ton cruiser converted in 1913. This ship was torpedoed and sunk by U27 on 31 October 1914.

Converted to the Commando role with Wessex 5 and Sea King A/S helicopters, the *Hermes* is seen below with a Harrier on deck during proving trials in the English Channel, February 1977.

The *Hermes* began a long association with the Borough of Tiverton in 1959, when the local Sea Cadet Corps was named TS *Hermes* to coincide with the commissioning ceremony. In 1968 the Borough adopted the carrier and on 19 July 1973, decided to confer the Freedom of the Borough on her: "... in recognition of the glorious achievements of the Royal Navy both in peace and war, and in appreciation of the close and cordial association which has existed in recent years."

Two former commanding officers were present at the ceremony – Vice-Admiral Sir Terence Lewin, KCB, MVO, DSC, (later First Sea Lord and CDS, Admiral of the Fleet); and Rear-Admiral D. G. Parker, CB, DSO, DSC, AFC.

At the time of writing, the *Hermes* is again being modified, this time with the angled ramp or ski jump, to permit operating the high performance Sea Harriers. With the *Invincible,* she is expected to be the first to operate these modern V/STOL aircraft.

In November 1934 it was announced that the new aircraft carrier would be called the *Ark Royal,* and she was laid down on 16 September 1935 at Cammell Laird, Birkenhead, and launched on 13 April 1937 by Lady Maude Hoare, wife of the first Lord of the Admiralty.

Originally designed to carry 72 aircraft, her nominal displacement was 22,000 ton with a length of 800 ft o.a. (244 m), a beam of 94¾ ft (29 m) and a mean draught of 22 ft (7 m). Armed with 16 4.5-inch dual-purpose guns, 6 multiple pompoms and 8 multiple machine-guns, she commissioned on 16 November 1938 under the command of Captain A. J. Power (later Admiral of the Fleet Sir Arthur), and was Flagship of the Vice-Admiral Aircraft Carriers, Vice-Admiral G. C. C. Royle, and then Vice-Admiral L. V. Wells.

On 3 May 1940, Captain Power was relieved by Captain C. S. Holland, who in turn was relieved on 19 April 1941 by Captain L. E. H. Maund.

Her war career was celebrated by the repeated German claims to have sunk her. She joined in the search for the *Graf Spee;* took part in the attack on the French Fleet at Mers-el-Kebir (Oran), and the expedition to Dakar. HMS *Ark Royal* then joined Force H at Gibraltar and took part in many successful operations, including the sinking of the *Bismarck.* On 14 November 1941, after being torpedoed the previous day by U81, she turned over and sank within sight of Gibraltar.

After 23 years' service, HMS *Ark Royal* arrived home for the last time on 5 December 1978 and berthed at Devonport flying her 450 ft (137 m) long paying-off pennant. The 50,786-ton (51,600 tonnes) carrier was the biggest warship ever to fly the White Ensign – a mighty floating airfield able to move 500 miles (800 km) in 24 hours, with the most flexible weapon system the Royal Navy ever had at sea.

Leeds adopted the first strike carrier on 4 November 1941, just 10 days before she was sunk. The adoption was to give incentive to 'Warship Week', and the loss of the *Ark Royal* prompted the citizens to raise the magnificent sum of £9.3 million (about £40 million today) towards the cost of the new carrier, and they adopted this *Ark Royal* before the keel was laid in 1943.

The delayed blow of losing our last strike carrier was lightened by the government statement that the third ship of the Invincible Class was to be named *Ark Royal*. This delighted the City of Leeds, whose remarkable loyalty to the carriers was demonstrated on 25 October 1973, when the Freedom of the City was conferred on the carrier.

At that ceremony, the Queen Mother mentioned the special place the *Ark Royal* also held in her heart. "I launched her twenty-three years

ago at Birkenhead and since then I have visited this great ship on all but one of her commissions." Recalling that the City had even longer ties with the *Ark Royals,* Her Majesty went on: "The ties of affection have prospered, and the granting of this honour gives the citizens of Leeds the opportunity to show their loyalty and devotion to those who have served and are serving their country with such loyalty and devotion." The Roll of Freedom was signed by Captain A. D. Cassidi, who was later relieved in his post as Flag Officer Naval Air Command by Captain Anson, on 5 January 1979.

When Captain Edward Anson rang down 'finished with engines' for the last time, a small piece of British naval history died. The name of the *Ark Royal* as a strike carrier spanned 41 years of naval aviation, and she was the last of a once mighty fleet of carriers who helped bring peace to the world. Her demise brought to an end traditional fixed-wing operational flying in the Royal Navy.

The *Ark* had left Devonport on 5 April 1978 for her last deployment overseas, which was to take her to the Caribbean, Florida, California, Greece, Italy, Majorca, Malta, Gibraltar and to the North Sea for exercise 'Northern Wedding', where she had her usual Russian snooper (below).

The six HAS2 Sea Kings of 824 Squadron were already embarked when she sailed and they were joined by the 12 Buccaneer S2s of 809 Squadron, 10 FG1 Phantoms of 892, 4 Gannet AEW3s of 849 'B' Flight and the 2 Wessex 1s of the Search and Rescue Flight. She was one of two large carriers included in the 1940 Supplementary Programme and on 7 February 1942, HM the King approved renaming the second of these (formerly *Irresistible*), the *Ark Royal*.

Laid down at Cammell Laird on 3 May 1943, she was launched on 3 May 1950 by the Queen Mother. 810 ft long (247 m) overall, she had a beam of 158 ft (48 m), and displaced 36,700 ton. She was fitted with a 5½° interim angled flight-deck and was commanded by the designer of this great British naval invention – Captain D. R. F. Campbell, who had also commanded 803 Squadron in the first strike carrier *Ark Royal* at the outbreak of the Second World War.

The *Ark* recommissioned on 1 November 1956 after an extensive refit with the angled flight-deck extended over the port side forward. She was fitted with all the latest aids for a Task Force Commander and the lubrication system of the steam catapult had been redesigned to minimize servicing.

On 30 July 1964, a new strike carrier CVA01 was announced to replace the *Ark Royal*, leaving the carrier fleet with CVA01, the *Eagle* and the *Hermes*. In February 1966, CVA01 plans were scrapped and the end of fixed-wing flying in the Navy was signalled in the Defence White Paper of 1968, which baldly announced that the carriers were to be phased out.

The new Conservative Government of 1970 was only prepared to delay the end of the big strike carrier by extending the life of the *Ark Royal*. On 24 February 1970, after a £32-million refit, she recommissioned under the command of Captain R. D. Lygo. The refit provided for modifications to the port catapult, and rebuilding and resiting the starboard one with blast deflectors. A fully angled flight-deck was fitted as in the *Eagle*. The upper portion of the hangar deck was stiffened to accept bigger loads, and there was a 199 ft (61 m) long catapult fitted on the port waist. The increased power of the catapult, due to a lengthened stroke, allowed the Phantoms to be launched in 'nil' wind conditions.

New direct-action arrester gear was fitted with greater energy absorption enabling bigger and heavier aircraft to be landed at higher speeds. On 11–12 May 1971, successful Harrier trials were conducted in the *Ark Royal* and she arrived back in Devonport at the end of July 1973 for a further refit, completed in 1974, designed to prolong her operational life to the end of the 1980s.

An unusual view of the upper and lower hangars.

Another feature of the last big refit was the bridle arrester gear seen in operation on the last ever launches of Phantoms from the catapults of the *Ark Royal*. Previously, the bridle linking the aircraft to the catapult was lost at the end of each launch. Now it was retrieved with significant economies and the elimination of a logistic problem. The bottom picture shows that the bridle has been retrieved.

One of the *Ark Royal*'s Phantoms shows its paces in a low-level strike role and below, a close formation combat air patrol of Phantoms.

This landing sequence illustrates clearly the tremendous strain put on the arrester wires when a Phantom, weighing 30,000 lb empty, is brought to a sudden halt.

This unusual picture shows a Gannet AEW3 of 849 B Flight flying at almost wave-top height, as it passed astern of a Royal Fleet Auxiliary.

The Sea King HAS2 of 824 Squadron demonstrates its anti-submarine strike role by launching a Mk44 homing torpedo. The current squadron commissioned on 24 February 1970 and took part in the *Merc Enterprise* rescue of 1974.

The *Ark Royal* as she will be remembered by the many thousands of officers and men who have sailed in her. This picture was taken during exercise 'Ocean Safari' in 1975, with her aircraft lashed down in adverse weather conditions. Held in the Eastern Atlantic and Norwegian Sea, 65 ships and 17,000 men from Canada, Denmark, West Germany, the Netherlands, Norway and the USA took part.

These imaginative pictures show the *Ark Royal* entering Valletta
Harbour and below, the 'worm's eye' view of a Buccaneer aircraft on
the *Ark*'s deck.

HMS *Ark Royal* leaves Valletta Harbour for the last time in November 1978 with Gannets, Sea Kings, Phantoms and Buccaneers ranged on deck.

Off Sicily on 27 November the last aircraft to be launched from the *Ark Royal* was crewed by Flight-Lieutenant Murdo Macloud, RAF (pilot), and Lieutenant Denis MacKelvie, RN (Squadron Deputy AEO). They flew off to RAF St Athan (below) where all the fixed-wing aircraft were handed over to the RAF immediately their engines shut down. During this last 8-month trip, nearly half of the fixed-wing pilots were RAF and HMS *Ark Royal*'s aircraft dropped a total of 60,000 lb of bombs and fired 14 air-to-air missiles.

With afterburners flaming, a Buccaneer as flown by Captain Anson, blasts of her pods of 36 2-inch rockets during a supersonic dive. The aircraft could do Mach 0.85 at 200 ft (562 knots at 61 m).

Captain E. R. Anson served as a pilot with 801 and 807 Squadrons (Sea Furies) during the Korean War and flew Sea Hawks with 800 Squadron during the *Ark Royal*'s first commission of 1955. He was Senior Pilot of 895 Squadron, HMS *Bulwark*, during the Suez Campaign, and after completing ETPS joined the Scimitar Intensive Flying Trials Unit (700X) before joining the *Victorious* as Senior Pilot of 803 Squadron (Scimitars).

After two years as a test pilot to the Blackburn Aircraft Company flying the NA39 Buccaneer he became Senior Pilot of the Buccaneer Intensive Flying Trials Unit (700Z), at RNAS Lossiemouth. In 1962, as Commanding Officer of 801 Squadron, he formed the first operational squadron of Buccaneers, embarking in the *Ark Royal* (January 1963) and then in the *Victorious*.

Promoted to Commander in December 1963, he later became Commander (Air) Lossiemouth, and in the *Eagle*. As a Captain, he

served as Naval and Air Attaché, Tokyo and Seoul 1972–1974. He assumed command of the *Ark Royal* on 28 September 1976.

Just before the *Ark Royal* paid off for the last time, it was announced that he had been selected for promotion to Rear-Admiral and appointment as FONAC, in June 1979. He joins a long line of distinguished Flag Officers who have commanded the two strike carriers, including Admirals of the Fleet Sir Arthur J. Power (1938) and Sir Peter Hill Norton (1959); Admirals Sir Michael Pollock (1962) and Sir Anthony Griffin, Sir Frank Hopkins, D. C. E. F. Gibson, M. F. Fell, R. D. Lygo and A. D. Cassidi.

This picture and others of the *Invincible* were taken during the extensive sea trials and are reproduced courtesy of Rolls-Royce Limited.

AN INVINCIBLE COMBINATION

On 17 May 1973, an order was placed with Vickers Shipbuilding Group, Barrow-in-Furness, for the first of a new class of 'through deck cruisers' operating anti-submarine helicopters.

On 15 May 1975, the Maritime Harrier was given the go-ahead and an order was later placed for 25 Sea Harriers FRS Mk1. On 24 May 1978, a further 10 were ordered.

First of the new ships was named HMS *Invincible* and she was launched by HM the Queen at Barrow on 3 May 1977, (below) without the ski jump. A Flight of three Sea Kings from 819 Squadron, Prestwick, and a Harrier from Vicker's airfield on Walney Island, flew over the ship in salute.

Now officially designated an anti-submarine carrier CVSOI, the *Invincible* is, like her sister ships HMS *Illustrious* and *Ark Royal*, a compact aircraft carrier of 19,500 ton (19,800 tonnes), with an overall length of 677 ft (206.6 m), a beam of 90 ft 3 in (27.5 m), a moulded depth of 70.5 ft (21.49 m) and a draught of 24 ft (7.3 m). Formally accepted by the Navy on 19 March 1980, she cost £175 million and commissioned on 11 July 1980 (Captain Michael Livesay).

She already has several 'firsts': the largest warship built for the Navy since the 1950s; the largest in the Western world powered entirely by gas turbines; the first purpose-built for aircraft and helicopter operations; and the first in the world with a ski jump. Contrary to popular belief, the carriers are not a panic reaction to the cancellation of CVAOI nor to the phasing out of the *Ark Royal*, but stem from a Naval Staff requirement of the 1960s for a 6,000-ton helicopter cruiser.

It was the invention of the angled ramp by Lieutenant-Commander D. R. Taylor that provided the invincible combination of ship and Sea Harrier. Like the *Invincible*, the *Illustrious* and HMS *Hermes* (now refitting) are expected to be fitted with 7° ramp. In the *Ark Royal* it is to be increased to 12°.

The 550 ft (168 m) long flight-deck is angled to port with the island bridge, twin funnels and radar sited on the starboard side. The two MacTaggart Scott hydraulic lifts are sited just aft of the island and forward, abreast of the fire control radar. They serve a three-deck-high hangar.

Following intensive flight trials at RAE Bedford with a Harrier operating from the ramp at angles up to 20° with remarkable success, the speed with which the invention was accepted into naval service – including the retro-refit of the *Invincible* – was without precedent. Design predictions indicate that with a 15° ramp at sea, typical take-off runs of 200 ft (61 m) would be reduced by two-thirds, and payload-radius of action doubled.

The first public demonstration of a Harrier operating from a ski jump was at the SBAC Farnborough Air Show 1978.

The ski jump is a simple device which increases the Short Take Off (STO) performance of vectored thrust aircraft like the Harrier. The aircraft has a reasonable payload under Vertical Take Off (VTO) conditions, but its performance is outstanding if allowed an STO of 80 knots or more.

With the ski jump, a short horizontal runway leads to an elevated ramp and the take-off is as in a normal STO until approaching the end of the ramp, when the nozzles are lowered to around 50 degrees. The initial flight path is angled upwards and the most immediate benefit is a quite dramatic reduction in take-off distance. With the ramp at 20°, this take-off distance is halved at normal take-off weight. The aircraft is in full wing-borne flight some hundreds of yards from the end of the ramp, and 200 ft higher 10 seconds later.

The Lieutenant-Commander proved the ramp theoretically during a sabbatical year at Southampton University 1972/3. The trials at RAE Bedford was conducted with experts from Hawker Siddeley's design team, who had also done extensive work on the project.

During its Service career, the Harrier has landed on 30 different types of warships and auxiliaries. This picture was taken during trials on the *Ark Royal* in 1971.

This picture was taken on the weekend of 2/3 August 1969 and shows the first-ever Harrier landing on a Royal Navy cruiser HMS *Blake*, on a flight-deck 117 ft (36 m) long and 56 ft (17 m) maximum width. These trials went a long way to convincing the Government that the Harrier would be a viable proposition at sea, after withdrawal of the *Ark Royal* and her aircraft. In an emergency the Sea Harrier could operate from a wide variety of merchant ships with or without the ski jump, and the three ships of the Invincible Class will be able to operate future Harriers fitted with 'supercritical wings', and to cross-operate with other friendly warships.

These first pictures of Sea Harrier aircraft carrying out operational trials in HMS *Hermes*, were taken in 1979 while she was in the Irish Sea. Aircraft Nos 100 and 101 were the first delivered to the 700A Intensive Flying Trials Unit at RNAS Yeovilton. Aircraft number 439 was from BAE Dunsfold, and numbers 440 and 450 from A & AEE Boscombe Down. The Boscombe Down systems aircraft 450 is armed with a gun pack, Sidewinder missiles and long-range fuel tanks. The frigate HMS *Euryalus* (seen right) is on plane-guard.

Shown above on an assembly line of Hawker Siddeley Aviation, the Harrier is still the Western world's only V/STOL aircraft in operational service. The Sea Harrier differs from the RAF's GR Mk3 in having a raised cockpit and a new design nose that folds to port for easy stowage.

On 18 June 1979 at the BAE airfield, Dunsfold, the first Sea Harrier XZ451 was officially accepted by the First Sea Lord, Admiral Sir Terence Lewin, on behalf of the Royal Navy. The aircraft is equipped with Ferranti's Blue Fox multi-role radar and an all-digital Nav/attack system. It went to 700A Intensive Flying Trials Unit, RNAS Yeovilton, which became 899 Naval Air Squadron with 6 aircraft on 31 March 1980 as the shore-based Headquarters Squadron. The first front-line operational squadron was also formed on 31 March 1980 and 800 Naval Air Squadron deployed in HMS *Invincible*, prior to joining HMS *Hermes* in late 1981. Two other front-line squadrons will be formed – 801 Naval Air Squadron early this year to serve in the *Invincible*, and 802 Naval Air Squadron to serve in the *Illustrious*.

The *Invincible* has COGAG – all-gas turbine – propulsion using four Rolls-Royce Marine Olympus TM3B turbines mounted in pairs, with a total installed horsepower in excess of 100,000, to give a speed of 28 knots. One engine in each pair is fed from a starboard air intake with the other two fed from the port intake. Engine pairs are driven through a David Brown triple-reduction reversing gear-box. Main engine controls are housed in the Control Centre. The TM3B module is of a simple and robust design, with a life expectancy well beyond that of the ship in which it is installed. The bold and imaginative step to opt for all-gas turbine propulsion in new construction warships, was announced by the MOD (Navy) Department in 1967, following successful trials in HMS *Exmouth*.

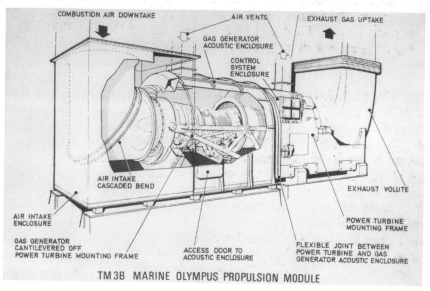

TM 3B MARINE OLYMPUS PROPULSION MODULE

A fine view of the *Invincible* showing the flight-deck angled to port and the ski jump. Below is a Sea Harrier about to lift off from the end of the ski jump.

Twin Scott 2 aerials, one fore and the other aft, provide satellite communications and the Marconi ICS3 (Integrated Communication System) provides comprehensive communication requirements on all other channels. A Marconi/Hollandse surveillance and target indicating radar is mounted on the forward aerial platform; a Marconi 9920 air and surface radar on the mainmast, and the domes fore and aft of the island are the Marconi 909 tracking and illuminating radars for Sea Dart. The *Invincible* has the most modern Action Information Organization (AIO) in the RN, within which is the ADAWS Mk6 with two Ferranti FM1600 computers.

The main anti-submarine weapon system is the Sea King helicopter which will be improved to the Mk5 standard, with a type 195 dipping sonar. The Westland Sea King carries four Mk46 torpedoes or four depth charges and has an automatic flight control system. Later, it is expected that these helicopters will be replaced with the EH101 (formerly WG34), a joint Westland/Augusta development, to replace the Sea King and SH3D helicopters in the Royal Navy and the Marina Militaire Italiana.

Scene in the hangar with Sea Harriers being maintained.

HMS *Illustrious* was launched by Princess Margaret on 1 December 1978 at the Wallsend Yard of Swan Hunter Shipbuilders Limited. Among guests attending the ceremony were Mr Fred Mulley (Defence Secretary), and Admiral of the Fleet, Earl Mountbatten of Burma. Like the *Invincible* which is fitted to Flagship standards, she will have a crew of some 900 and her aircraft complement will be five Sea Harriers and nine Sea Kings.

The 1980 Defence White Paper confirmed that a feasibility study had been completed into the possibility of updating the Harrier with a 'big wing' to give it improved range, load and manoeuvrability. The wing is designed to fit the RAF's present GR Mk3.

The Sea Harrier FRS1 first flew on 20 August 1978 and 34 have been ordered for the Navy, together with a T4 two-seat trainer. They derive from the GR Mk3 but are powered by a Rolls-Royce Pegasus 104 vectored thrust turbofan of 21,500-lb (9,752 kg) thrust, to give a speed in excess of 640 knots. It can reach Mach 1.25 in a shallow dive (Mach 1 is 760 mph (1,398 km/h) at sea level and a pressure of 1,033 millibars). Intercept radius is 400 n. miles (750 km) and strike radius 250 n. miles (450 km). Maximum weapon load 8,000 lb (3,630 kg).

The Sea Harrier has a wing span of 25 ft 3 in (7.7 m), length overall 47 ft 3 in (14.4 m), nose folded 42 ft 6 in (12.95 m), and a height of 12 ft 2 in (3.7 m).

Formerly designated the P3T, this second generation all-weather, air-launched, sea-skimming anti-ship guided weapon under development by British Aerospace Dynamics Group, has been named Sea Eagle. It will arm the Sea Harriers and the RAF's Tornados and Buccaneers. Sea Eagle has an active radar homing head and a computer. Before firing, the weapon computer is supplied with target position information from the launch aircraft, and controls the weapon flight path to impact. The computer uses micro-processors. It is powered by an air-breathing gas turbine developed by Microturbo, Toulouse, and has a good operational range. Development and initial production is funded by UK MOD.

At the time of the 1980/1981 Defence Estimates in April 1980, HMS *Invincible* was working up; the Commando Carrier (ASW) HMS *Bulwark* was in reserve; the Assault Ship HMS *Intrepid* was in commission. HMS *Hermes* and the Assault Ship HMS *Fearless* were doing long refits and the Helicopter Cruiser HMS *Blake* is now scrapped. The ASW carriers HMS *Illustrious* and *Ark Royal* were building.

Naval Aircraft 1980/1981

Fixed Wing	Role	Deployment	Squadrons	Flights
Sea Harrier	FRS	HMS *Hermes*	1	
	Aircrew Training	Yeovilton	1	
Helicopters				
Sea King Mk2	ASW	HMS *Hermes*	1	
		HMS *Bulwark*	1	
		HMS *Invincible*	1	
		RFA's	1	
		HMS *Gannet* (Prestwick)	1	
	Training	Culdrose	1	
Lynx Mk2	ASW	Leander, Type 21 and 22 Frigates and 42 Destroyers		18
	Training	Yeovilton	1	
Wasp	ASW	Leander, Rothesay and Tribal Classes, 21 Frigates		25
	Training	RNAS Portland	1	
Wessex Mk3	ASW	County Class		2
	Training	Portland	½	
		Portland	½	
Wessex 5	Commando Assault	Yeovilton	2	
	Training	Yeovilton	1	
	Aircrew/SAR Training	Culdrose	1	
	FRU	Portland	1	
Sea King Mk4	Commando Assault	Yeovilton		1

248

Bibliography

Air Aces of the 1914–1918 War, Bruce Robertson, Harleyford Publications, 1959.
Aircraft of World War 1, Kenneth Munson, Ian Allan Ltd, 1967.
Airship in Peace and War, The, J. A. Sinclair, Rich & Cowan 1934.
Armament of British Aircraft 1909–1939, H. F. King, G. P. Putnam's Sons, 1971.
Avro Aircraft Since 1908, A. J. Jackson, G. P. Putnam's Sons 1965.
Bristol Aircraft Since 1910, C. H. Barnes, G. P. Putnam's Sons, 1964.
British Naval Aircraft Since 1912, Owen Thetford, G. P. Putnam's Sons, 1977.
British Rigid Airship, The, 1908–1931, Robin Higham, G. T. Foulis & Co. Ltd, 1961.
British Airships, The Father of, Alec McKinty, William Kimber & Co. Ltd, 1972.
British Aeroplane, The, 1914–1918, J. M. Bruce, G. P. Putnam's Sons, 1957.
Fights and Flights, Air Commodore C. R. Samson, Ernest Benn Ltd, 1930.
Four Ark Royals – The, Lt-Cdr Mike Apps, William Kimber & Co. Ltd, 1976.
From Sea to Sky, Sir Arthur Longmore, Geoffrey Bles Ltd, 1946.
Hurricats, The, Ralph Barber, Pelham Books, 1978.
Naval Air Service, The, 1908–1918, Captain S. W. Roskill, DSC, MA, Naval Record Society, 1969.
Naval Eight, edited by E. G. Johnstone, Arms and Armour Press, 1972.
Naval Operations, Sir Julian Corbett, Longman Group Ltd, 1920.
Seaplanes – Felixstowe, Gordon Kinsey, Terence Dalton, 1978.
Ships of the Royal Navies, Oscar Parkes, Gale & Polden, 1937.
Sopwith – The Man and His Aircraft, Bruce Robertson, Harleyford Publications, 1970.
Vickers – A History, J. D. Scott, Weidenfeld Ltd, 1963.
Zeppelin in Combat, The, Dr D. H. Robinson, G. T. Foulis & Co. Ltd, 1962.

Some Fleet Air Arm Trophies

Boyd. Premier annual award for the finest feat of naval aviation. This silver model of a Swordfish commemorates the work done for naval aviation by the late Admiral Sir Dennis Boyd, who captained the carrier *Illustrious* at Taranto in 1940, and in 1945 became the first Admiral (Air), RNAS Lee-on-Solent.

Dunning Memorial. Commemorates the achievement of Sqn Cdr E. H. Dunning, first British naval pilot to land on the deck of a ship under way. Wg Cdr Longmore and brother officers purchased the trophy privately. In 1921 it was awarded to Flying Officer W. F. Dickson (later MRAF Sir William) and after being held in trust by the Air Council, it was returned on 6 December 1966 to RA D. W. Kirke, FONFT. It is now held at the FAA Museum, Yeovilton.

Kelvin Hughes. Awarded annually to A/S Unit most efficient in assessment and conduct anti-submarine operations. First awarded 1971.

Sandison 1972. Awarded annually to aircrew making the most valuable contribution to weapon development and tactics. Donated by Mr and Mrs Paul Sandison in memory of their son.

Australia Shield. Awarded annually to the squadron making most progress in operational efficiency.

During the early days on the Navy News Desk, MOD, the author and his colleagues were frequently asked by students set essays or other tasks, about the early history of the FAA. These dates are as accurate as can be ascertained.

Chronology 1908–14

1908	3 June	Captain R. Tupper informs Director of Naval Ordnance, Captain R. H. S. Bacon, that two Petty Officers and four Leading Seamen are at Farnborough training on Cody's Kites.
	21 July	Captain Bacon (later Admiral Sir Reginald) asks 1SL for post of Naval Air Assistant to be created; liaison with War Office and construction of a rigid airship. Proposals accepted.
	14 August	Vickers, Son & Maxim asked to tender for building rigid airship R1.
	17 August	Cody at HMS *Excellent* doing trials with man-lifting kites for observation. One reached a height of 1,700 ft (518 m).
	23 October	CID set up Advisory Committee for Aeronautics. Members include RA Sir C. L. Ottley and Captain Bacon.
	6 November	Captain Bacon reports only practical use for kites was to widen horizon for scouting.
1909	28 January	1909–1910 Estimates CID recommends £35,000 for building R1.
	31 March	CID recommends experiments with aircraft be terminated and advantage taken of private enterprise in this field.
	1 May	Special Air Branch formed to oversee building R1 – members Captain Murray Sueter, first Inspecting Captain of Airships; Cdr Oliver Schwann (Swann), Lt C. P. Talbot, Lt N. F. Usborne, Chief ERA Sharpe. Borne books of HMS *Hermione*.
	7 May	Vickers tender accepted for R1.
1910	21 June	Lt G. C. Colmore, first NO to qualify as a pilot at his own expense. Certificate No. 15.
	6 December	General Fleet Order promulgated that Mr F. K. McClean will lend two aircraft free to teach NOs to fly.

1911	17 January	Vickers inform Admiralty they could produce under licence a French machine to take off from HM Ships. Admiralty refuse offer.
	2 March	Lts C. R. Samson, R. Gregory, A. N. Longmore, and Captain E. L. Gerrard, RMLI, report for training at Eastchurch. Later joined by Captain C. Wildman-Lushington, RMLI. Instructor Mr G. B. Cockburn. Borne books HMS *Wildfire*.
	1 April	Army Air Battalion formed to train an expert body of airmen.
	25 April	Lts Samson (Certificate 71), Longmore (72) and W. Parke, who was trained Hendon, (73) qualify as pilots after less than six weeks' training.
	2 May	Lt Gregory qualifies as pilot (75) and Gerrard (76).
	30 May	Lt Richard Bell Davies qualifies as pilot (certificate 90).
	29 September	R1 named *Mayfly* broke her back.
	October	Samson persuades Admiralty to purchase two training aircraft from McClean and detail 12 ratings for Eastchurch. Borne books HMS *Actaeon*. Admiralty agrees to lease 10 acres near Royal Aero Club, Eastchurch.
	18 November	Cdr Swann made first British take-off from water in Avro biplane bought and converted at his own expense. He was not a qualified pilot and aircraft crashed on landing.
	18 November	Technical Sub-Committee formed to study aviation Army/Navy. Members included RA Sir C. L. Ottley, Samson, Gregory and Captain M. P. Hankey, RMA.
	1 December	Lt Longmore flew modified Short S27 with flotation bags from Eastchurch and landed safely on River Medway.
1912	2 January	Lt Hugh Williamson, a submariner who had qualified as a pilot (Certificate 160 28 November 1911), submitted a paper entitled 'The aeroplane in use against submarines'.
	3 January	Admiralty close down airship construction.
	10 January	Samson flew Short S38 off platform built over bows HMS *Africa*. Aircraft landed safely on water. First British take-off from a warship.
	27 February	Technical Sub-Committee recommend setting up RFC with Army and Naval Wings.
	13 April	RFC constituted by Royal Warrant.
	16 April	Cdr Swann awarded certificate 203.
	7 May	Longmore appointed HMS *Hermes* for command Cromarty Naval Air Station which then existed only on paper.
	9 May	At Fleet Review Samson flew modified S27 off *Hibernia* steaming at 10½ knots. First British take-off from ship under way.
	13 May	Naval Wing becoming known as RNAS with about 22 officers, 8 with pilot certificates. Captains Sueter, Paine; Cdrs Swann, Samson, Masterman; Temporary Major Gerrard and Captain R. Gordon, RMLI; Lts Gregory, Usborne, L'Estrange Malone, Boothby, Seddon, Woodcock, Parke, S. D. Gray, Fitzmaurice; Eng.-Lts E. F. Briggs and C. F. Randall. Also borne on books ERA F. W. Scarff, inventor of Scarff ring and gun mounting.
	19 June	CFS opened Upavon with Captain Godfrey Paine as first Commandant (to date 25 July).
	1 July	Admiralty recommends purchase Willows No. 4 'blimp' which went to Farnborough in October as HM Naval Airship No. 2. Later modified Farnborough as SS1.
	15 July	Referred to as Military Branch RN. Seniority list gave Sueter, Paine, Swann, Masterman, F. R. Scarlett, E. M. Maitland, Samson, Usborne.
	17 August	First course Upavon with six RN/RM officers.
	25 September	Naval Airship Section reconstituted at Farnborough with Masterman, Usborne, Boothby and Woodcock attached Airship Squadron, Military Wing, to gain experience.
	10 October	Admiralty approved chain of Naval Air Stations round our coasts.
	November	Air Department set up at Admiralty with Sueter first DAD assisted by Swann, L'Estrange Malone and Eng.-Lt G. W. Caldwell. Samson appointed to command Naval Flying School, Eastchurch.
	11 December	First naval flying fatality when Parke killed in crash.

251

	31 December	Lt Seddon commissioned Isle of Grain as first naval seaplane station.
1913	10 April	Lt Spenser Grey commissioned Calshot.
	13 April	Lt Gregory to HMS *Actaeon* additional as Sqn Cdr to command Yarmouth Group of Air Stations and Lt C. L. Courtney as Flt Cdr Yarmouth Air Station.
	15 April	Great Yarmouth Air Station commissioned.
	24 April	Scarlett qualified as pilot (No. 468).
	7 May	HMS *Hermes* (Captain Vivian) commissions in succession to HMS *Actaeon* as HQ RNAS.
	10 July	Historic Fleet manoeuvres, first time aircraft operated with the 351 ships taking part.
	17 July	Winston Churchill announced in House use of word seaplane for aircraft taking off from sea.
	21 July	Short Folder No. 81, first aircraft with folding wings flown off forward platform *Hermes* by Samson.
	13 August	Air Department first General Orders refer to *Hermes* as parent ship Naval Air Service (first time this term used). Captain Vivian in charge all Naval Air Stations.
	2 September	All ranks RNAS transferred to books of *Hermes* except those at CFS borne books HMS *President*.
	1 December	Naval Depot, Sheerness as HQ RNAS.
	5 December	Administration now under 4SL Captain C. F. Lambert (later Admiral Sir Cecil) and first mention need for Naval Air Service Training Manual.
	20 December	Lt Travers designed clockwork bomb-sight which could be fixed to aircraft.
	31 December	Captain Scarlett (later AVM High Speed Flight which won Schneider Trophy 1927) appointed in general charge Naval Air Stations as first Inspecting Captain of Aircraft, Naval Air Office, Sheerness.
1914	1 January	Army Airship Branch disbanded and airships transferred to RNAS.
	15 January	Longmore took command of Calshot from Spenser Grey.
	17 March	Churchill told House there were 103 naval machines of which 62 were seaplanes. Of 120 regular pilots 20 held RAC certificates. There was one PO pilot and 540 men.
	31 May	Lt A. W. Bigsworth pilots seaplane for Maxim gun trials on flat target towed by HMS *Nubian*. Fires 200 rounds with 60 hits.
	4 June	Lt T. S. Cresswell, RMLI, killed in seaplane crash when overflying Solent.
	23 June	RNAS as separate entity was to consist of Admiralty Air Department, Central Air Office, Flying School, Eastchurch and Air Stations. New ranks introduced starting Wing Captain (Captain RN).
	1 July	RNAS formed and lasted until the formation of the RAF in 1918.
	18–22 July	Spithead Review. Flights of seaplanes took part from Isle of Grain (Sqn Cdr Seddon), Dundee (Sqn Cdr Gordon, RMLI), Felixstowe (Sqn Cdr Risk), Great Yarmouth (Sqn Cdr Courtney) and Calshot (Sqn Cdr Longmore). 19 aircraft took part including Short Folders, Farmans, Sopwith Tractor and Tabloid, BE2s, Avro biplane, Bristol Scout, Sopwith Bat Boat and 50-hp Short.
	28 July	Sqn Cdr Longmore (later ACM Sir Arthur) made first successful torpedo drop from Short seaplane at Calshot. It weighed 800 lb (364 kg) and was 14 inches in diameter.
		Fleet ordered to War Stations.
	29 July	Churchill minutes DAD primary duty of aircraft to fight enemy machines. They are not to be wasted on ordinary scouting duties.

Index

255